ROUTLEDGE LIBRARY EDITIONS:
JUNG

Volume 1

DRAWINGS FROM A DYING CHILD

DRAWINGS FROM A DYING CHILD

Insights into death from a Jungian perspective

JUDITH BERTOIA

Routledge
Taylor & Francis Group
LONDON AND NEW YORK

First published in 1993

This edition first published in 2015
by Routledge
27 Church Road, Hove BN3 2FA

and by Routledge
711 Third Avenue, New York, NY 10017

Routledge is an imprint of the Taylor & Francis Group, an informa business

British Library Cataloguing in Publication Data
A catalogue record for this book is available from the British Library

ISBN: 978-0-415-82179-7 (Set)
eISBN: 978-1-315-75425-3 (Set)
ISBN: 978-1-138-79115-2 (Volume 1)
eISBN: 978-1-315-76300-2 (Volume 1)
Pb ISBN: 978-1-138-79517-4 (Volume 1)

Publisher's Note
The publisher has gone to great lengths to ensure the quality of this reprint but points out that some imperfections in the original copies may be apparent.

Disclaimer
The publisher has made every effort to trace copyright holders and would welcome correspondence from those they have been unable to trace.

Drawings from a dying child

Insights into death from a Jungian perspective

Judi Bertoia

ROUTLEDGE
London and New York

First published 1993
by Routledge
11 New Fetter Lane, London EC4P 4EE

Simultaneously published in the USA and Canada
by Routledge
a division of Routledge, Chapman and Hall, Inc.
29 West 35th Street, New York, NY 10001

Typeset in 10 on 12pt Palatino by LaserScript Limited, Mitcham, Surrey
Printed and bound in Great Britain by
Biddles Ltd, Guildford and Kings Lynn

British Library Cataloguing in Publication Data
A catalogue record for this book is available from the British Library.

Library of Congress Cataloging in Publication Data
Bertoia, Judi
Drawings from a dying child : insights into death from a Jungian perspective / Judi Bertoia.
p. cm.
Includes bibliographical references and index.
1. Terminally ill children–Psychology–Case studies. 2. Children and death. 3. Children's drawings–Psychological aspects. 4. Jung, C.G. (Carl Gustav), 1875–1961. I. Title.
RJ249.B47 1992
155.9'37–dc20 92-15267
CIP

ISBN 0–415–07218–2
0–415–07219-0 (pbk)

This book is dedicated to Caroyl
who became a child of my heart, a teacher as well as a student
and who is remembered with love

In the midst of winter
I finally learned there was in me
invincible summer

Albert Camus

Contents

Illustrations

PLATES

TABLES

Acknowledgements

This book represents contributions from many people. They have touched my life and influenced the material contained in these pages. While I wish to express my gratitude to all of them, there are a few individuals who deserve special acknowledgement.

The very existence of the book is a reflection of my family. I am grateful to my parents Henry and Barbara Schellenberg for their encouragement to be open to learning, faith and humanity. My husband Wayne and children Richelle and Kevin have shared the pain of loss and the joy of creation as this material became part of our lives. I am grateful beyond words for their continuous love and support.

I am particularly appreciative of all that I have learned from two of my teachers, both very talented men. Gregg Furth has taught me a great deal about myself, drawing interpretation and death. John Allan, who was also my university supervisor and head of my thesis committee, has provided constant encouragement for my professional and personal growth. My thanks also go to my thesis committee, to Larry Cochran for his research suggestions, and Bob Steele for his encouragement to extend the work.

For their generous contributions in time, energy and expertise I am indebted to Stan Auerbach, Gwen Buker, Suzanne Elliott, Diana Livingston, Bruce Morley, Mary Ann New, and Cory Roach. A special acknowledgement goes to Maureen Argatoff for her insightful suggestions on the manuscript. I applaud Bay Gumboc for her outstanding work typing the manuscript and Ed Montgomery for his sensitive reproductions of the drawings. Thanks also to those at Routledge, in particular to David

Stonestreet, Andrew Samuels, Anne Gee, Bradley Scott, Jo Thurm, Katy Wimhurst and Hugo de Klee.

I especially want to thank Doug and Carol Lindsay. Their capacity to love is a gift, their ability to cope an inspiration. Finally, I am grateful to Caroyl. Her incredible spirit continues to teach us through her drawings. Caroyl's legacy has been a profound gift.

The drawing which appears on plate 32 is also the cover of *Inscapes of a Child's World* by John Allan, 1988, Dallas, Spring Publications. The poem 'The Flame' on p.10 is reprinted with permission from *Living With Death and Dying* by Elizabeth Kübler-Ross, 1981, New York, Macmillan. Eleven of the drawings and some of the details of picture analysis in the book were previously included in 'Counselling seriously ill children: Use of spontaneous drawings' by J. Bertoia and J. Allan, 1988, *Elementary School Guidance and Counselling*, 22: 206–21. © ACA. Reprinted with permission. No further reproduction authorized without written permission of the American Counseling Association

Chapter 1

Children and death

In society today there is a much greater trend towards open discussion of death and the dying process than there was twenty, or even ten years ago, and yet a pervasive discomfort with the topic still exists. The reality of death is brought home nightly in evening news. Death is televised to us from Eastern Europe, Tian An Men Square, and the Middle East. Increasingly, the number of deaths and fear of death from diseases such as AIDS has forced many adults to face their own mortality. But in spite of this increased exposure, some people still tend to repress the thoughts and emotions death arouses. The desensitization that comes with viewing carnage in movies such as *Rambo* and *Total Recall* fuels the fantasies of invincibility that many people entertain, just as the re-appearance of many 'dead' performers in the visual media perpetuates a wish to deny personal mortality. While there has been a trend to more open discussion of death and to more support for the dying and their loved ones, such as the hospice movement and bereavement groups, many adults retain a fear, a wish to avoid both the dying and the bereaved.

Their discomfort is often intensified when death involves a child, whether that child is grieving a loss or is terminally ill. Many people avoid the topic with children, believing this avoidance protects the child. Other people think children do not understand death, and so there is no need to talk with them about death issues. While children's understanding of death does depend on many factors such as age and experience, they do know some of what has happened and will create their own version of circumstances when not told. Perhaps even more disconcerting is the thought that children do know when they are dying. If no one talks to them about it, what can they use to fill in the blanks; what frightening experiences do they create in their imaginations?

In response to concerns such as this, many people are beginning to look at ways of gaining greater insight to children's experience of life-threatening illness and to what is helpful for them. Several authors have indicated that terminally ill children do, at some point in their disease, know they are dying. Elisabeth Kübler-Ross provides several examples of children expressing this knowledge either in symbolic, nonverbal language (drawings and play) or in symbolic verbal language depending on their age. A few are even able to clearly verbalize their knowledge, 'I know I'm going to die very soon and just have to talk to somebody about it' (Kübler-Ross 1981, p. 21). The child who made this statement was eight years old.

Myra Bluebond-Langner, an anthropologist, studied hospitalized, terminally ill children and writes about her discovery that those children progressed through five stages of changing self-concepts, finally viewing themselves as dying (Bluebond-Langner 1978). These changes were expressed through their behaviours and language. In some cases the awareness of being near death was overtly stated, depending on previous interactions with the adults involved. Bluebond-Langner found that what the children were able to clearly communicate depended strongly on their perceptions of adult expectations of them and on what any given adult could tolerate. In *There is a Rainbow Behind Every Dark Cloud*, several children have worked together to write about their experiences with potentially fatal diseases and they say:

> It was hard for most of us to talk about how we felt inside. And it was hard for us to find someone who would really listen without being afraid. Sometimes the questions we were afraid to ask were: 'Am I going to die?' 'What is dying like?'
> We knew certain questions would bring tears to our parents' eyes so we learned not to ask those questions. All of us seemed to want to protect our parents.
> At the same time, we wanted to be physically close to our parents most of the time. Lots of times we didn't want them out of our sight.
>
> (Jampolsky & Taylor 1978, p. 31)

Bernie Siegel describes a two-year-old in his book *Peace, Love and Healing*. During the child's final hospitalization, he was able to tell his mother 'I'm going to be a little bird soon and fly off. I wish you could come with me, but you can't' (Siegel 1989, p. 232). A few weeks later, this same child indicated he wanted a kiss on either cheek from Dr Siegel, a privilege never before permitted his doctor; he died fifteen minutes later.

Susan Bach has been working in this field for decades and has repeatedly found that children's drawings reveal both their psychological understandings of what is happening and their physiological state. She uses the phrase 'it knows' indicating that even before the children are consciously aware of their prognosis and revealing it in their symbolic verbal language, their art indicates a pre-conscious knowledge of their illness and its outcome (Bach 1969). She uses this information to assist the child and family in dealing with the impending death when that is appropriate for their needs. Keipenheuer (1980) and Furth (1981) have written of similar findings and the use of drawings with critically ill children.

Bach, Keipenheuer, and Furth all advocate the use of drawings with children to determine what they know about their disease. Some children, especially older, verbal children may be able to articulate what they already know and what they still find confusing, but many cannot. This inability to express themselves may be a result of being socialized into not acknowledging their awareness, or it may simply indicate their lack of verbal skills to bring the topic into the open. There are also some children who should not have discussions go beyond their feelings about their illness. By 'reading' a child's drawings, Bach believes those adults involved can help the child at the appropriate level of need. Kübler-Ross writes,

> Spontaneous drawings reveal the same information a dream will reveal. It can be obtained in a few moments in almost any environment – hospital, school, or home. It costs simply a piece of white paper and coloured pencils. It sheds light within minutes on the preconscious knowledge of children and adults – a tool simple and inexpensive and easily accessible, as long as we have enough conscientious therapists who have been trained in the interpretation of this material.
>
> (Kübler-Ross 1981, p. 17).

Allan describes the value of using drawings with children for a variety of problems, including terminal illness (Allan 1988). Having children draw permits the expression of inner issues in a way that can easily be shared with another. This sharing allows those adults willing to talk with a child an opportunity to gain some insight about what is significant for the child at the moment. Equally important, it also allows the adult to see what is happening from the child's view, and hopefully thereby avoid adult projections into the child's work.

When there is an opportunity for serial drawing, that is, for the child to meet alone on a regular basis with a supportive adult for creative activities, Allan believes the child's unconscious material is more readily expressed in symbolic form (Allan 1978). This consistent, expressive opportunity activates the healing potential of the psyche, thus permitting the terminally ill child access to inner resources for coping with problems, including death.

Rando reviews the literature on the awareness of terminally ill children and writes that it is a moot issue whether or not these children can comprehend their own death, but it is necessary for adults to help them with their feelings and with whatever understandings they do have. She refers to the loneliness and fear a terminally ill child feels with no one to talk to about the disease and prognosis (Rando 1984).

Given that terminally ill children do have some understanding of and emotions related to their dying, and that many adults are unwilling to talk to them about it, it is important that those who are willing, be effective and understanding of what the child needs. It is also important to understand the experience of a dying child. Because children's pictures reveal their inner experience, this book will describe what that experience may be, as indicated in one child's drawings.

This book evolved from the author's experiences as a home/hospital teacher in the Canadian school system. While teaching she was also pursuing her Master of Arts degree in counselling psychology. One of the children she was asked to work with at that time, a seven-year-old named Rachel, had been diagnosed as having chronic granulocytic leukaemia. Following this diagnosis the family had moved from their small community to the metropolitan area to be closer to Children's Hospital, a major pediatric referral centre in the province.

Although Rachel was able to complete second grade at school, by third grade it was decided she would receive home/hospital teaching. The author's primary task was to teach Rachel language arts and maths during their daily, one hour sessions. Other subjects, such as social studies and art were included if Rachel felt well enough. At that time, one major initiative within the school district was the creative writing process. The activities in this subject area suited Rachel well because in addition to loving maths, she really enjoyed creating. The poems, stories, and pictures contained in this book are nearly all from these academic pursuits. However, because Rachel drew so frequently, a few of the images she created for her family are also included in order to enrich and clarify Rachel's message about dying and death.

During those daily, one-to-one school sessions throughout third and part of fourth grade, a strong bond developed between Rachel and the author. This relationship facilitated the other main principle of home/hospital teaching, that of helping to support the child through the stressful times of being seriously ill. Simply having school, like healthy children do, is part of the psychological value of home/hospital programmes but there are times when counselling issues predominate. Rachel directed some of the discussions to even more penetrating, philosophical levels at times. One such discussion led to her writing the following poem:

I Wonder

I wonder why a bunny rabbit has such a fluffy tail
I wonder about the people who make the ingredients for
the gingerbread man
I wonder why we get thirsty so often in a day
I wonder why there's colours when it could be
black and white
I wonder why people use only 9 per cent
of their brain, not ninety
I wonder why God made the world

Rachel later decided to include this poem in her creative writing project, a book which she entitled 'Rachel's Life' and planned as her last Christmas gift for her family.

Rachel was also a very open child, usually bubbling with the joys of life. At that time the author was unfamiliar with the psychological value of drawings but on one occasion became interested in a discrepancy between one of Rachel's pictures and its title. When asked if it could be shared with other counselling psychology students, Rachel replied, 'Judi, you can share any of my stuff with anybody you think should see it!'

Rachel retained a philosophical attitude until her death in January, 1986. In 1990, the author wrote a study of Rachel's creative work for her Master of Arts thesis. That material, in turn, has become the foundation of this book. The author hopes to describe Rachel's experience so that readers will gain some insight as to how she became fully aware she was dying and even came to accept death. Rachel's story is one of great joy and great pain and the legacy she has left is profound.

Organization of the book

The next chapter summarizes current theory related to children's awareness of their illness and dying, as well as the therapeutic use of drawings with children in general. Chapter 3 details the rationale for a case study approach and describes the procedures used for collecting the information presented in this book. There is also a discussion of the technique used for in-depth analysis of picture content. Chapter 4 presents the analysis of a set of drawings along with convergent material related to this child. Chapter 5 provides a discussion and summary of the patterns which emerged in the analysis and addresses the comments and queries raised by the physician assisting with medical interpretations and by the family. It also discusses the themes which emerged from the analysis and the implications for theory. Suggestions in the final chapter are intended for caregivers – medical personnel, clergy, teachers, counsellors, mental health workers – and for families with a dying child, offering practical strategies for coping. For those who are interested, the appendices contain information from the original research where experts in the field of drawing interpretation were asked to categorize each of the drawings (Bertoia 1990). Also, there is a glossary to assist the reader with some of the less common terms which are used frequently in this book. Hopefully, by sharing the information contained in this book, readers will find themselves a little extended in their knowledge of life and of death.

Chapter 2

Current theory

Over the past three decades, the volume of literature discussing death and children has been slowly increasing. Some aspects of current theory are especially pertinent to the concepts presented in this book. In order to explore what children's awareness of dying is, one must have some understanding of just how children express themselves. Also, it is useful to have some idea of how children develop an awareness of their own imminent death. At the present time, two views of this awareness process are widely acknowledged. One way to gain an understanding of this world of children is through their drawings, just as using case studies is one method for investigating the human experience in depth. The material in this chapter describes children's awareness of dying and how they express it, as well as the use of drawings and case studies with critically ill children.

Children's awareness and expressions of dying

Although a great deal has been written about children's cognitive understandings of death (Betz & Poster 1984, Matter & Matter 1982) and about the care of terminally ill children (Van Dongen-Melman & Sanders-Woudstra 1986, Rando 1984), the intent of this section is to review the actual awareness and understanding that terminally ill children have about their own dying process.

Rando's survey of the literature (1984) indicates that before the 1970s, two common beliefs were: (a) that children, for a variety of reasons, should be protected from the knowledge of the complete truth about their disease, and (b) that most children did not know, in an adult sense, that they would die and so were not concerned about it. Since that time there has been increasing evidence that terminally ill children do have an understanding of their prognosis and also have strong emotional responses to it. Rando indicates that caregivers should operate on the assumption that children do know and therefore, open communication should be encouraged. Her findings also indicate that although there must be communication with children, it should be in the context of their ability to understand, as well the appropriateness of the information from the family's viewpoint.

In their very comprehensive literature review, Van Dongen-Mellman and Sanders-Woudstra (1986) also found this current encouragement for openness based on the recognition that the child is aware, but they are much more critical of the need for this communication to be done effectively. They note that very few of those providing empirical evidence are able to describe exactly what constitutes effective communication. However, they do cite some authors who provide details about the use of play, art, groups, counselling and drawings as vehicles for helping children cope with the disease, prognosis, and intense emotional reactions. In spite of the vast amount of existing information on the psychosocial aspects of childhood cancer they reviewed, they still conclude there is a further need for new knowledge of the child's course of becoming aware of the life-threatening aspects of the disease.

Kübler-Ross, who by 1981 had been working almost exclusively with dying children, writes, 'Small children, even three- and four-year-olds, can talk about their dying and are aware of their impending death' (Kübler-Ross 1981, p. 51). In this sense 'talk' is at one of three levels of language children use. She explains that there is a clear verbal level, 'You know Mommy, I feel so sick now that I think this time I'm going to die' (Kübler-Ross 1981, p. 59). While this child was only four at the time and survived until he was nine, his history and experience with illness allowed him to understand even at that young age and to verbalize his awareness. A seven-year-old girl, near death, repeatedly asked different adults what it was going to be like, 'when I die', until she found an adult who would even talk with her about it.

The second level of expression is a symbolic verbal level, the message uses words but is much less clear until the context is understood. A parent who was convinced her twelve-year-old son had not talked about dying found the following poem 'The Flame' after his death:

The flame is like a human,
It lives and dies.
Its life span is a wild impetuous one
During its span – it frolics dances and
Appears to have a carefree existence.
Although it might be joyous in a short period
It has a tragic death
The tragedy is in its struggle not to die.
But first the flame casts an eery bluish magnetism
Just as it's about to let go, it flickers and springs
Back to life again.
At that moment it appears that the vital desire
For survival will be the victor.
But neither flame nor human is destined for eternal life
Death is near – the flame sputters as it reaches out to
grasp on to a dangling string, trying to resist its
overshadowing fate – but to no avail . . .
Death has exhausted its opposition
And conquered!

(Kübler-Ross 1981, p. 61)

In the chapter 'Children's Inner Knowledge of Death and Their Symbolic Language', Kübler-Ross (1983) cites a great many poems, stories and dreams related by children which clearly indicate their knowledge.

The third form of communication is through nonverbal symbolic language, which consists of drawings, play, and symbolic gestures. Kübler-Ross describes an angry, depressed thirteen-year-old who had been waiting, in hospital, over a year for a donor kidney. His constant behaviour of pretending to shoot little girls was distressing the nursing staff and upsetting the other children. When she spoke to him, he replied, 'Did you notice I not only pick little girls, but they all have good kidneys?' (Kübler-Ross 1981, p. 19). Bluebond-Langner relates the story of a child who in her play took paper dolls, which she had earlier said looked like her, and buried them, and said: 'Put them in their grave, in the Kleenex box. Let me do it' (Bluebond-Langner 1978, p. 185). Also, she tells of a little boy known for his art work who suddenly drew only graveyards. These then are examples of nonverbal symbolic language. All these forms of symbolic language – behaviour, play and art – can clearly indicate the child's awareness of strong emotions and death.

The group of children aged eight to nineteen who wrote *There is a Rainbow Behind Every Dark Cloud* describe their experiences, emotions and coping strategies as they faced life-threatening illnesses. They found it helpful to talk about death and their emotional responses, with other young people when adults were uncomfortable, and to draw pictures, because the reality of the images made death less frightening. This group was very open about their awareness and obviously the group support was helpful.

Furth believes that dying children are able to reach a sense of completeness prior to death even if it is not expressed in adult terms. He indicates that the child's level of awareness about the disease is indicated in drawings. Part of his training was with Susan Bach in London who began work in this field in the 1930s. Her approach has been to interpret the drawings, and only then have the doctors involved in the medical care of the individual share the case history. Her great detail in the analysis and cross-checking, as well as her wealth of knowledge, have made her a valuable and respected source in this field.

Bach states her strong belief that there is a link between the psyche and soma (psychological and physiological self). In her article 'Spontaneous paintings of severely ill patients', she demonstrates this linkage by analysing the drawings done by two critically ill children. She appends one hundred and fifty colour figures so the reader can follow the detail she presents. Bach concludes that this material offers visible proof that, deep within, every patient knows whether there will be recovery or death. She very supportively writes to those who have difficulty accepting this material,

> I should like to say to the reader of this paper: if what the children tell us in their drawings awes you and you would rather not have it true, be assured that we too who have worked on them for so many years still find our hair stand on end and breathless silence befall us . . . .
>
> (Bach 1975, p. 102)

The linkage between mind and body is especially important at critical moments in a child's life and, when the life is threatened, the psyche reacts (Bach 1969, Furth 1988). Keipenheuer has used children's drawings in his medical practice as an additional tool to better understand both the physiological and psychological status of his young, critically ill patients. Siegel also believes in this connection, and being a surgeon considered scientifically how the actual link occurs. He cites a neuropeptide theory advanced by Candace Pert and others which suggests the neuropeptides 'as the locus where mind and body meet and cross over' (Siegel 1989, p. 102). Pert also proposes the physiological location of the conscious and the unconscious and goes on to consider emotional states and disease.

> Psychologists talk about deep subsconscious processes. Clearly the network of chemicals that I have attempted to describe suggests that the subconscious extends to one's T-cells, to one's monocytes, and, in a kind of flowing way, back to one's brain cells.
>
> Freud also made important observations about how emotional status could contribute to disease status. In this context it seems to us appropriate to consider that with all the circulating neurojuices – and all the neuropeptides can be found in different proportions in different organs throughout the brain, the glands, and the immune system cells – we are seeing a constant aqueous solution that makes a continuum of the brain and body.
>
> (Pert with Dienstfrey 1988, p. 193)

Bach (1969), Keipenheuer (1980), Furth (1981), and Siegel (1989) all use the interpretation of drawings to decipher what is happening for the child and all believe children are aware if they are dying.

Models of understanding

Bluebond-Langner (1978) studied children hospitalized with leukaemia and believes this awareness of dying develops over time. She explains there is a changing view of self which results from the synthesis of information and disease experience. There are five stages of acquisition of factual information about the disease:

1 'it' is a serious illness
2 names of drugs and side effects
3 purposes of treatments and procedures

4 disease as a series of relapses and remissions (-death)
5 disease as a series of relapses and remissions (+death)

The children need concrete information and experience before they move to a different stage. They need to know the names of drugs and their side effects and they get that information through personally experiencing the disease which necessitates those treatments in the first place. Secondly, they need the experience such as nosebleeds or relapse to relate the information to their own situation. The acquisition of information is cumulative and the stages are sequential, progressing from diagnosis or 'well' on through stages 1 to 5 with no reversal in sequence. Although there is a transition time as they move closer to the next stage, the children are not identified as being in the next stage until they have both information and experience from the previous stage. This is also true of the five stages of changes in self-concept:

1 seriously ill
2 seriously ill and will get better
3 always ill and will get better
4 always ill and will never get better
5 dying (terminally ill)

The integration and sequence is explained in more detail below using the labels which indicate the level of awareness.

Stage 1: Seriously ill

The children have been admitted to hospital for tests, a bewildering and frightening experience for children and families. At first, children view themselves as 'normal' children, expected to behave as other children, using typical childhood techniques for getting what they want. Following diagnosis based on their history, physical examination and test results, the children quickly become aware of the differences in how adults act towards them and of how many more gifts they receive. This leads to a new view of self as being 'seriously ill' which is demonstrated by an 'exhibition of wounds', where every visitor is shown the pricks from needles, on every visit. The children's separation fears at this point are more of the unknown and unfamiliar rather than of the final prognosis. This view of self persists until there is evidence they are getting better; usually it takes four consecutive clinic visits, 'consultations' with other children, and confirmation from their mothers that they are in remission.

Stage 2: Seriously ill and will get better

From regular out-patient clinic visits the children learn of various drugs and their effects, usually from conversations with other children. They do not pass into Stage 2 until they have experienced a remission and a few rapid recoveries from disease related incidents such as nosebleeds and headaches. Once they have passed into Stage 2 the drugs have made them feel better and most people treat them normally again. The longer they are in remission, the more they believe that they will eventually get better. They essentially see themselves as sick before, but better now.

Stage 3: Always ill and will get better

Following the first relapse the children are required to reframe their thinking of themselves. They have begun the chronic relapse–remission cycle and the familiarity of symptoms and procedures return. There had been a time, perhaps a long time where a return to 'normalcy' pushed the realities of the disease well into the background. They find that adults will not talk to them about the disease or the drugs, so they resort to eavesdropping on the adults and discussing symptoms, drugs and side effects with the other children. At the same time they need people, especially adults, around them. Adult reactions of avoidance and discomfort require the children to learn appropriate social roles for maintaining the essential, supportive contacts. They come to associate their symptoms, the painful medical procedures and adult reactions of avoidance and tears with a view of themselves as being always ill, but that at some future time they will ultimately get better. Once they are in remission again, the parents and consequently the children come to believe that one can be sick many times, but one can still recover.

Stage 4: Always ill and will never get better

More relapses, on-going pain, and sometimes drug complications, force the children to see themselves differently. Their decreasing abilities, their greater removal from normal childhood activities, and the increasing hospitalizations create the sense of having better times and worse times, but always within the context of 'being sick' times. They can do less and less for themselves, planning for the future stops or becomes very short term; they no longer think in terms of 'what I want to be when I grow up' or even of distant holidays, they mourn the developmental stages they will not experience.

Stage 5: Dying

Once children are in stage 4 they may stay there for some time; but hearing about the death of a peer from the same disease, causes them to move into Stage 5.

They realize the remission – relapse cycle has a definite end, death. However, they cannot synthesize this information until they are themselves in Stage 4, so that earlier deaths from the same disease will not have this effect. It is necessary for them to accumulate all the disease and treatment knowledge personally before this disastrous new awareness can take place. Their activities and interests now tend to have limited themes, often symbolically reflecting death. In various forms, either overt statements, or through symbolic verbal and nonverbal images, the children indicate that they know they are dying. For many, the cause of death of these others was a major focus, as was the similarity of that cause to their own circumstances.

Communication becomes more of an issue at this stage. For many children there is a need to protect the adults, to maintain a form of mutual pretence. This is simply a way of each knowing what will happen but not communicating this knowledge. In order to cope on a daily basis there is a pretence between adult and child that everything will get better. This keeps the needed adults close and allows for relief from constantly dealing with the intense emotions. There is decreasing communication with people and less cooperation with many procedures, especially painful ones which have not made any positive difference so far. For many children there is an awareness of time, of not being here indefinitely and of not wasting time now. Bluebond-Langner indicates the transition from Stage 4 to 5 can be over hours or over months, depending on the circumstances, but ultimately all children end up at Stage 5 at an inner level, knowing and expressing their awareness of their own personal death in some form.

Kübler-Ross (1983) deals with a more spiritual aspect of children. She believes that all terminally ill children become aware that they are dying, but cautions that for some children this awareness may be pre-conscious rather than a conscious, intellectual knowledge. She also believes that children who are hospitalized frequently or for long periods grow up more quickly than children who do not experience life threatening illness.

A nine-year-old with leukaemia asked her what death was like. Her reply to him was a letter which was ultimately printed for ready access to others. In the beautifully illustrated 'Dougy Letter' (1979) she drew 'Man' as a circle with four quadrants, each representing one aspect of the individual: intellectual, physical, emotional, and spiritual/intuitive. She believes that the child's awareness of death 'comes from the "inner, spiritual, intuitive quadrant" and gradually prepares the child to face the forthcoming transition, even if the grown-ups deny or avoid this reality' (Kübler-Ross, 1983, p. 134).

In her workshops Kübler-Ross explains these quadrants. Typically, they mature as part of the normal developmental stages of a child. She explains that children develop the physical quadrant in the first year of life. From ages one through six the emotional quadrant develops, and then the child is ready to approach the intellectual one with enthusiasm at about age six, often coincident with entry to academic pursuits associated with formal schooling. The fourth quadrant, the spiritual/intuitive one, generally develops during the teen years (Kübler-Ross, 1985). She also explains that one quadrant can enlarge, using more than its 25 per cent share at the expense of another quadrant. It can happen because an individual is concentrating on one aspect of life, such as a time when intellectual or physical activities dominate one's life in school, athletic training or work, or because something dramatic happens that changes an individual's focus in life. However, as death approaches, the spiritual component enlarges, especially if there is a gradual debilitation of the body as the disease progresses causing a natural diminishing of the physical quadrant. This concept accounts for the unconscious aspect of human nature and adds a greater depth of understanding to the dying process than is described in Bluebond-Langner's five stages.

Kübler-Ross (1969) writes that terminally ill adults slowly separate from interest in this world as death approaches, the time of letting go or 'decathexis'. At this time the dying still want an assurance they will not be left alone, but they may not want a lot of visitors and there will be decreasing interest in the events of the world and activities of the visitors. Near the very end they may want only nonverbal communication, the quiet holding of a hand or just the physical presence. Those who accepted death tended to die without fear and despair, with a form of acceptance or resignation, especially when helped with the monumental task of separating from everything. In Kübler-Ross's experience, those who fight the disease and maintain a battle attitude until the very end may not have this acceptance and she cautions caregivers to be aware of how they interact with the patient. It is essential that the patient's attitude guide all exchanges and that helpers respect the patient's needs and style of functioning in the world. Caregivers who attempt to force their own beliefs or style onto a patient would only make the ending much more painful.

Even as they are letting go of their attachment to all they hold dear, many dying individuals express belief in a life beyond their existing form. This belief may be referred to as 'going home' to be with their God or loved ones, or it may be understood as existence through the effect one life has had on others. More frequently, this new awareness of the self continuing, although in some altered form, is expressed in a symbolic manner such as through dreams, art, poetry, or verbal references. These images indicate a new beginning, a 'rebirth'. Being more conscious of this rebirth potential seems to help individuals cope with the impending and absolute separation while at the same time nurturing hope and love.

Use of drawings

As indicated previously, Bach (1969, 1975) has used drawings as a basis for communication with terminally ill children for years. They provide a glimpse of the child's innermost, personal self. She writes:

> To a child, the form he paints, a house, a flower, etc. is not just a shape, it is **his** house, **his** flower: they are an expression, an equivalent of himself. He may draw, for instance, his favourite

> toy horse being irradiated precisely at the spot where he himself had been X-rayed that very morning: the picture reflects his own condition.
>
> (Bach 1969, p. 16)

By providing an awareness of what is happening for the child, pictures can direct adult interactions in the way which will be most helpful to the child. Hammer (1985) expresses this same view, adding that children find it easier to communicate, especially those things they will not or cannot share verbally, through drawing. Hammer reminds us that children draw before they can write, and he continues by saying that drawings, like dreams, indicate the projected content of our unconscious conflicts. 'Drawings, like symbolic speech, tap primitive layers of the subject' (Hammer 1958, p. 7). Furth (1988) provides and analyses examples of drawings from children and adults drawn at a variety of critical times. Allan (1988) provides detailed case studies of how drawings have been used to help children deal with a range of traumas including physical and sexual abuse, divorce and terminal illness. Each of these writers bases their approach on the assumption that what the child draws comes from deep within, and represents aspects of the whole child.

Drawings have been used in the clinical setting for many years as projective techniques (Hammer 1958). They have been used as a tool to aid in medical diagnosis (Bach 1969, Keipenheuer 1980, Siegel 1989). In addition, they are commonly used now to assist children and adults with expressing and healing psychological wounds (Allan 1988, Allan & Bertoia 1992, Bach 1975, Furth 1988, Wohl & Kaufman 1985).

Analysis of drawings

When undertaking the interpretation of a drawing, one must be very cautious about what one says (Allan 1988, Furth 1988). There is always the danger of reading into another's creation that which is, in reality, only a part of one's own psychology. There is also a need to be tentative, for each drawing is a unique creation, reflecting the one who drew it. The image may appear to be one thing to the viewer, yet is something quite different to its creator; the monster may turn out to be a favourite stuffed animal. In working with children, it is often very useful to discuss the drawing in the third person, especially in the initial phases of therapy.

Different approaches to deciphering a drawing include concentrating on the images and emotional response they elicit (Allan 1988), following a series of guidelines (Bach 1977, 1990) or working with a series of focal points (Furth 1988). As one becomes more involved with the drawing, an awareness of the images tends to lead the reader into the drawing, as if one were part of it.

These images come from within the one who created the picture, yet there is frequently a commonality with other images created throughout human history. Susan Bach writes:

> Pictorial reflections of basic human experiences are relatively limited in number and, as C.G. Jung has shown and we have found confirmed in critically ill patients' drawings, are fundamentally the same everywhere, irrespective of race, place, or time, though they can be modified in detail by the individual or different environments. Being even older than writing, such pictorial key signs can be taken as the letters of man's universal alphabet. The symbols of such basic powers, once recognized, can thus be traced and translated.
>
> (Bach 1990, p. 66)

Krippner (1989) examined a wide range of religious and mythological death imagery and concluded that a common thread is the sense of power over death through a theme of death and rebirth. Jung also indicated that

> As a rule the approaching end [death] was indicated by those symbols which, in normal life, also proclaim changes of psychological condition – rebirth symbols such as changes of locality, journeys, and the like.
>
> (Jung 1960, p. 410)

Standard symbol dictionaries (Cooper 1978, The Herder Symbol Dictionary 1986) can provide useful information for interpretation as can common dreams related to the subject of death (von Franz 1986). Thompson and Allan (1987) provide some possible interpretation of common symbols used by children, and Bach (1969) and Furth (1973) provide insights into the colour preferences of leukaemic children. Di Leo (1983) shares many insights into the drawings of latency age children, and Kellog (1969) catalogues typical drawn images from pre-school children.

Case study approach

The case study approach seems most preferred for research about children and drawings in this field (Bach 1975, Keipenheuer 1980). It allows for the inclusion of many pictures as a supplement to the on-going history. Keipenheuer (1980) obtained more than three hundred drawings from one leukaemic child over three years. As the child's doctor he found the material contained in the drawings to be most valuable for treating the child and for helping the family deal with their own grieving process. By appending reproductions of the drawings, both he and Bach provided an opportunity for others to follow the interpretations. Because both of these examples are from Europe, consideration must be given to cultural differences when making comparisons between North American drawings and the images presented in their case studies.

Furth (1973) was unable to find any material in North America similar to Bach's and Keipenheuer's when he was conducting his own research comparing the content of drawings by leukaemic children with those of other children, some of whom were hospitalized but not with life-threatening situations and some of whom were healthy. In his study each of forty-five children drew three pictures over a period of three months. While his findings were not statistically significant, there were distinct trends. Leukaemic children tended to draw indoor scenes, not to fill in their main objects and not to draw suns – but when they did draw them the suns tended to be positioned differently. Healthy children tended to draw faces on their suns.

A second part of Furth's research was to have a panel of three art professionals analyse the sets of drawings. They concluded that analysis was difficult because of the similarities in the drawings. Two of the three panellists also indicated intuitively that there was something different between the leukaemic children's drawings and the other two groups, but could not be specific. The third part of the research was a case study and in his conclusion Furth stated that,

> Case study techniques are more effective for evaluation technique as compared to statistical analysis or panel analysis in this type of work because it takes into account the whole child and not just one element of information regarding his works.
>
> (Furth 1973, p. 143)

While there is a growing body of literature about death awareness in children, much remains to be learned. The subsequent chapters of this book explore the relationship of existing theory with information derived from the works of one dying child.

Chapter 3

Tools for understanding Rachel's art

The experience of Rachel, a young girl dying of leukaemia, is the focus of this book. The art she created in her last few months leaves an opening for others to follow along her pathway because her work permits insights into the changes she underwent as she was dying. This chapter describes how Rachel's material was used as a map for directing others towards an understanding of her experience.

Rationale

The book undertakes a longitudinal, in-depth study of the experience of this little girl. Underlying this approach is the uniqueness of having so many drawings from such a child, for they reveal a great deal about her inner world. These drawings came into being as a natural part of her schooling at home; they were part of her daily routine, as school is part of any child's experience, thus they were not created experimentally for a study nor as part of her more traumatizing hospital experiences. A case study approach allows a rare opportunity to explore the complexities and depths of a child's view as a dying process unfolds.

To understand an individual's experience as fully as possible, it is necessary to take sufficient time to examine each available piece of evidence and to have that evidence as unbiased as possible. By using a longitudinal case study format, it was possible to investigate a variety of sources to enhance the understanding of Rachel's inner world. Although the book focuses on the in-depth interpretation of her drawings as the primary source, information from the medical charts recorded during periods of hospitalization was also used. Examining both the clinical findings and the comments of hospital staff who contributed to the charts provides the reader with a broader understanding of Rachel's condition. A third source of information about Rachel's physical and mental status was a transcript of an interview between Rachel's mother and the author. The interview, based on the personal journal kept by Rachel's mother during her daughter's illness, provides quotations from Rachel herself, comments from other family members and doctors, anecdotes of Rachel's behaviour, perceptive insights about her daughter's emotional status and indications of the changes in the disease. Thus, a comprehensive case study format allows for many sources of information to be integrated, and for many individuals to contribute their perspectives on the experience of this child as her short life ended.

Data collection

The data from the child, the teacher, the family and the hospital are used with the in-depth picture analysis. The drawings and the accompanying text for each are supplemented by teacher notes. In this case, the author was a participant-observer because her involvement at that time was as a teacher. This meant there was an opportunity to be directly involved on a regular basis and view the situation from the inside, yet there was no thought of doing any research at that time so that the observations noted were part of the teacher's daily log and were not planned as part of a research project. The parent interview was open-ended, specific dates and events were shared from the mother's journal, and both parents' thoughts on the understanding of children's death awareness were expressed. Archival evidence from the hospital was also made available.

Drawings

Of the sixty drawings collected from Rachel, all but one were done in her home. Every school session was held in Rachel's bedroom. She became very possessive of this time and even asked her mother to leave if she stayed very long after escorting the teacher into the room. Because her room became her 'school-room' for that year and a half, it was a very comfortable setting for Rachel, both for the drawings and for the more challenging maths, writing and other school projects. Only the very last picture was done in the hospital. Much of Rachel's time was spent with her large, loving family whose faith formed a strong, although never intrusive, basis for living. Extended family, neighbourhood friends, and many of those who came into professional contact with Rachel also became an increasingly important part of her world.

Following some difficulties with Rachel attending school in the second grade, her family requested that a home/hospital teacher be provided for her schooling the next year. She had had home schooling briefly with another teacher the previous spring when it was not possible for her to go to school, but she wanted to finish grade two with her friends. She completed all of the third grade and part of the fourth with the same home/hospital teacher who was then a part-time student at the University of British Columbia.

Creative writing, a major initiative in the school district at that time, made the language arts component of the programme easily accommodated at home. Initially, much of the work was based on showing Rachel a picture about which she then wrote a story. Later it was changed so that she drew a picture and dictated the story to go along with it. As her health deteriorated more and more, the picture was often drawn but with no story required. This came about mainly because of one particular experience with drawing.

One day, Rachel was feeling very sick but no phone call reached the teacher in time to cancel the session. When the teacher went into the bedroom, Rachel was asked if she felt able to draw a picture since the teacher was there anyway. She agreed, drew it, said the title was 'not feeling well', but wrote, 'not feeling bad'. When the teacher asked for clarification, Rachel said she felt much better after drawing the picture, adding 'I got it all out in the picture'. Rachel then requested her regular school session. This incident was shared with Rachel's mother and it was agreed that from then on, drawing alone was of value, and would continue as part of the school day whenever Rachel chose it.

Although sixty drawings were received from Rachel, only twenty-eight will be analysed in depth in this book. These were all collected between February 1985 and January 1986. Rachel gave all sixty of these drawings to her teacher along with her permission to share them with anyone the teacher felt should see them. Before any of Rachel's material was shared, permission was also obtained from both of Rachel's parents. This sharing seems to add some meaning to Rachel's death.

There were other drawings which were done for special occasions for her family. For both Christmases while she was receiving teaching at home, Rachel also created a 'book' for her family. These creative writing activities were printed on a computer, illustrated, and bound. They were very special to the family and the final page of the second book, which she titled 'Rachel's Life', was a poem so powerful that the family framed it and placed it on the casket at her funeral. This poem, written spontaneously one school day in November, indicates her strong belief and strength of spirit.

Up on a hill
There is a place for me
I know. Because the Bible
Tells me so

Rachel's creative works have since touched many people in many ways.

Most of the time Rachel was simply asked if she would like to draw a picture. Usually she would go ahead and complete one; these were the impromptu drawings (ones done on request but with no specific stimulus). Sometimes she was asked to create a drawing about a specific topic, such as a guided imagery activity she had just completed; these were directed drawings. Frequently, she would chat as she drew. If she was silent as she worked, so was the teacher. Following the drawing, the teacher would ask if it had a title or story and Rachel would dictate these. Sometimes the teacher simply asked if Rachel could tell more about a particular part of the drawing. The teacher made notes of the session on the back of the picture either during the discussion or immediately following the school session.

A few times, Rachel had drawn a picture the night before, completely on her own; these are the spontaneous drawings. Although she apparently did a great many of these, most were given to members of her family and only a few are included in this book. Any time a drawing was done within the school context she had the same materials with which to work, the only exception being different quality and size of paper some of the time.

Medical records

With the written approval of both the family and the attending primary physician, the author was able to review Rachel's medical records at Children's Hospital. A doctor accompanying the author made notes of pertinent details so that following the author's in-depth analysis of the drawings he would be able to assist with an understanding of what Rachel's medical status was at the time of any given drawing or on the admissions nearest the date.

Parent journal

Although the author had several contacts with the family following Rachel's death, no formal records were kept until over two years later when the original research was being planned. In June, 1988, Rachel's parents met with the author to discuss some specific events and dates. This interview also includes the sometimes painful, sometimes joyous story of a family's experience when a young child is dying.

Picture analysis

Using the principles suggested by Furth (1988), the following questions are addressed during the interpretation of each of Rachel's drawings:

1. What is the main focal point in this picture, i.e. what draws one's attention first?
2. What is odd in this picture?
3. Are there any barriers such as walls or fences?
4. What is missing?
5. What is central or in the middle?
6. Is there anything out of proportion?
7. Are there lines in the drawing, across the top or bottom or under any images?
8. Is there any edging, i.e. is part of an object off the page?
9. Are there erasures? If so, what is the effect?
10. Is there shading?
11. What colours are used, omitted, or out of place?
12. Is anything out of season?
13. Does the back of any drawing show extra pressure?

14 Do words appear in any drawings?
15 Are there any repeated objects?
16 What are the trajectories of objects, and what would the consequences be if they moved?
17 Are there abstract images?
18 Are objects filled in or empty outlines?
19 What images or symbols are there related to death, disease, future or view of self?
20 What feelings does this picture evoke in the viewer?

Responses which are clear are reported, but those which are not relevant in the drawing are not addressed. For example, question 3 asks if there are any barriers, but if there are none in a specific drawing, then that question is not mentioned in the analysis. Addressing only the pertinent questions reduces the volume of the book, and according to Yin (1989), a common complaint about case study research is the massive size of the report. For each drawing there is an in-depth analysis which is followed by the author's classifications for it according to Bluebond-Langner's model and according to the spirituality concept of Kübler-Ross, here broken into categories labelled 'decathexis' and 'rebirth'. (See Glossary and Appendix B for information on these terms.)

Convergent material

Following the analysis of each picture, the convergent information from the medical records and from the parent journal is presented for the readers' consideration. Thus, both conscious and unconscious images, both psychological and physical information, both subjective and objective content contribute to the insights available from this material, guiding the reader through Rachel's experiences.

Chapter 4

Rachel's journey

Just as a listener can never fully 'know' the subjective experience of another person's life or dreams, a viewer can never be certain of the meaning in another's drawing. Although a survey of picture content does help the viewer grasp some of the artist's status at the moment of creation, there are many possibilities and many levels to consider. Thus, the interpretations presented in this chapter are not absolutes but only the best thoughts of the author after much deliberation and with great respect for the unconscious and the individual creative process. Having stated this cautionary note, the chapter continues with an analysis of Rachel's drawings.

Picture analysis

Each drawing is referred to first by a number which is based on the chronological sequence of this series. The number is followed by the drawing's title, if Rachel gave it a title. While each story and relevant teacher notes appear within the text, comments and notes are also reproduced in their entirety in Appendix A should the reader want more detail.

Drawing 1 The first picture was drawn February 19, 1985. The focal point is the girl. She is the central image and most of her body stands under a cloud. All of the images are outlined, and a variety of coloured felt tip markers were used. A light brown colour outlines her face, and the light yellow hair is barely attached to top of her head. Both the eyes and legs are the same light blue colour and both the right eye and leg seem smaller. Her mouth is open in a rather lopsided smile. On either arm is a brown spider.

There are four oddities in this drawing. The outlining of the cloud in two colours, first blue, then yellow is unusual in children's drawings. The markings on the dress, described by Rachel as 'lines from running', and the position of the legs are also odd. Finally, the size of the tree trunk compared to its foliage is out of proportion. Since this was drawn in mid-February, the green foliage on a deciduous tree is out of season. The story which accompanies this drawing reads as follows:

> I'm walking in the forest and it's the last part of the forest and I see this bush walking up to me and I know it was Andrea tricking me. Then I saw Derek up in the tree. Then I thought, 'Andrea is playing a bad trick and any minute she'll jump up.'
>
> So then I went over to the bush and looked in and I saw Andrea. She said, 'How did you know I was here?'
>
> I said, 'I didn't.' And then I saw Derek and he asked how I knew he was there and I said I didn't. Then they put spiders all over me and I screamed all the way home.

This story indicates that as the girl leaves the forest, which is often thought of as a symbol of the unconscious, she intuitively knows to look into the tree and a bush approaching her. She believes the people hiding there [teenagers whom Rachel knew] are playing a 'bad trick' on her. When they put spiders on her, she runs home screaming.

In spite of the bright colours and apparent smile which initially suggest a cheerfulness, the text reinforces the drawing's image of physical weakness and helplessness in the face of bigger opponents who are seen as tricking and threatening her. Because it is drawn out of season, there is some significance to the tree. If the large tree trunk depended on the small amount of foliage for photosynthetic energy, it would not be healthy. The odd, bent angle of her legs would suggest a difficulty in supporting her. The spider represents the Greater Weaver or Creator (Cooper 1978, p. 156) who spins the thread of life. The picture was initially drawn without hands on the girl, suggesting a sense of powerlessness, and without the spiders; they were added after the story was dictated. The lines all over the clothing make the sweater-dress look as if it is unravelling, suggesting her thread of life is coming undone.

The initial feeling of brightness does not quite mask the underlying fear and denial. Because this is one of the few drawings with a text written in the first person, the image of a girl under a cloud who has just had spiders put all over her elicits intense feelings of foreboding in the viewer. This drawing can be classed in the category of Decathexis where there is a recognition of decreasing energy and danger, as if she intuitively knows there is a grave threat to her health yet wishes to deny it. Although there is a view of self as being seriously ill, in isolation this picture cannot be specifically placed according to Bluebond-Langner's stages because there are not enough indications of Rachel's disease experience and knowledge, nor of her future expectations.

Medical records

Rachel had been transferred from her home town to Children's Hospital in the spring of 1983. Her diagnosis at that time was chronic granulocytic leukaemia. Over the next two years she had been treated for the leukaemia and the following information was recorded near the date of these drawings. Rachel was hospitalized again in January of 1985. She had been experiencing night headaches, vomiting, and a urinary tract infection. Physical examination of the eyes revealed swelling of the optic nerve and small haemorrhages indicative of increased intracranial pressure, but other cranial nerves were reported as normal. Her blood tests showed a normal haemoglobin, a depressed white cell count and a decrease in platelets. A spinal puncture revealed 95 per cent blast cells in the cerebrospinal fluid (CSF) which was markedly elevated, and indicated active disease. She received Methotrexate intrathecally (injected into the back) for the first time. During the month she continued to receive out-patient treatments. Consideration was given to cranial radiation but it was not used.

Her mother is quoted as saying 'She was completely changed' for the better by the third chemotherapy treatment. Social worker comments quote Rachel's mother saying that Rachel knew she had a serious illness and that she would not get better, and also that she had expressed a fear of leaving her parents and family should she die. Later, she received Vincristine and ARA-C (cytosine arabinoside) also. By February 15, 1985, her bone marrow examination indicated she was in remission, although blood test results showed the marrow was chronically depressed.

Parent journal

Beginning in the spring of 1984, Rachel had great difficulty sleeping, often staying awake until 2:00 or 3:00 a.m. yet still trying to attend school the next morning. She often had nightmares, frequently of spiders. The family consulted with the hospital psychologist who agreed with their decision to have someone sleep with her. The conversation which decided the issue confirmed her mother's belief, 'and she said it so quickly, "I am afraid to go to sleep because Mommy," and at that point she began to cry, sobbing, and she said, "I am scared I am not going to wake up in the morning." '

As early as the fall of 1984, when she was seven, Rachel was speaking of dying. On September 21, 1984, in a conversation with her mother, Rachel said, 'When I feel sick I want to go to heaven. You know, like Calgon taking it away [a current advertisement on television] . . . When I die I'll see Grandpa.' On November 15, 1984, with an older sister she said, 'I can die you know.' Her mother wrote that Rachel was 'going to reverse the role of child and she was going to be the mother' which happened commonly with Rachel and many other children they saw in hospital whenever a parent or any adult seemed to have difficulty with what was happening. On December 3, 1984, with another sister she said, 'when I die I want to ask God a few things. I want to know if I can be guardian angel, if I can hug and hold little kids' hands when they need it.' The sister asked if Rachel's guardian angel hugged her and she replied, 'Oh yes, only if I am alone can I feel him. If I ask him, "Please hold my hand", I can feel his hand in mine and I can feel his hugs.'

On December 29, 1984, two weeks after her eight birthday, she had a long conversation with her mother,

> I wish I were in Heaven, then I wouldn't have leukemia . . . . I could come back and not have it . . . . I am so worried because my friends have died and I think I might die and I don't want to leave my family . . . . Promise me that if I die before you and Daddy that you and Daddy will be buried beside me.

In January 1985, Rachel had her first lumbar puncture and her mother had again recorded how wonderful the staff were, especially two doctors and a few of the nurses. Her journal entry summarized events as follows: 'They found leukemia cells in her spinal fluid and for the next five weeks Rachel was in and out of hospital for treatment.' Rachel experienced a lot of nausea and several headaches from the treatment and towards the end of it, one of the children to whom she had become very attached died.

On February 15, 1985, Rachel and her mother were working on a jigsaw puzzle and Rachel asked, 'Mommy, am I going to die? Did someone tell you I am going to die? Mommy, just answer me yes or no.' Rachel was very insistent about an answer, not just that her disease was not curable, but a specific response. Her mother describes the family's very strong belief that it is important not to lie, yet to still maintain the child's hope, a very difficult balance to achieve. Her mother gave examples of 'things she had said months before she was even diagnosed' which indicated Rachel had some intuitive knowledge of her future and her mother had written, 'That she [Rachel] was in contact with something far beyond what we even understood at that particular time.' They believed very strongly to reply 'Yes, you will die,' would 'destroy the human spirit within her' that was so necessary for coping with all the pain and procedures and that such a blunt response would have precipitated an early death. They also believe that Rachel lived many months longer because of her strong will and hopefulness.

Drawing 2 Created February 21, 1985, this picture's focal point is the wolf. This central image is outlined in brown and partly filled in with chaotic lines, heaviest on the top of his head. He has what appears to be blue saliva dripping beside a red tongue. He looks straight ahead, to the left of the page and if he kept walking he would pass right by the hiding children. The text tells us he is hungry, presumably he would devour them if he could. Both his right foreleg and hind leg appear smaller than the other side or are out of proportion, indicating that mobility could be a problem.

The oddity is the series of faces, each inside a circle, on one of the four trees. The children are hiding from the wolf here, and all four circles extend beyond the actual tree trunks, almost severing them. Two faces look frightened but two do not appear as much so. There are nine trees, five without a child in danger and four with a child in hiding from the wolf. All the trees are deciduous yet are in full foliage in February.

There is a feeling of danger, fear and chaos in the drawing. The lines on the trees go around in spirals and circles. The lines on the wolf and grass are drawn as if in haste, and go in all directions. The text indicates that the children were playing a game of hide-and-go-seek in a forest and then were frightened by a very real danger, the hungry wolf. An unidentified 'it' frightened the wolf also. Perhaps the 'it' which frightened the wolf was seeing an aspect of death, for symbolically the wolf has spiritual as well as helpful associations (Herder 1986), but is traditionally seen as a dangerous predator in Western fairy tales. In fact, the wolf goes away and never returns according to the story:

> These litle kids were playing hide-and-go-seek in the forest and all of them hid in a tree because a hungry wolf was coming by. And they were scared and ran away and it scared him too. And he never came back again.
>
> There's a hole and those are the holes in the trees where the kids are hiding.

The threat of the wolf goes away and never comes back again. The children hide in the trees from one danger and it goes away, yet four of the trees are almost severed by those circles. It could be that on one level there is a hiding from or denial of the disease, yet on a deeper, still unconscious level, there is already an awareness that the disease will be fatal. In the child's game of hide-and-go-seek, if you can stay hidden you are safe because you can run 'home free' while the person designated 'it' is away seeking others. In this story the game becomes real when the wolf approaches. First the children hide but then run away, thus never reaching the safety of 'home free'. By Bluebond-Langner's stages it would seem that Stage 3 'Always ill but will get better', here reflected as 'can hide and run away', could be an appropriate placement, but that on another level Decathexis or death awareness exists.

Medical records

No new entry.

Parent journal

Following her friend's death, Rachel seemed to have a period of prolonged anger lasting nearly three months. It was focused primarily on her mother and seems to have been a time of great turmoil.

> her anger period . . . all of a sudden everything I did was wrong . . . and I think what triggered it was the death of [her friend] . . . and now the anger is coming out because at that point she says, 'I didn't know I could die from leukaemia,' when she heard. She was already going through, I think, phase 3 into 4 [of Bluebond-Langner's model] when that happened. She was going through such a mixture . . .

Drawing 3 In this drawing of February 26, 1985, the face of the crying girl is both the focal point and what is odd. It is out of proportion and distorted. All the features are drawn in the bottom portion of the face. This picture is drawn with a vertical orientation of the paper, and is the only one in the series which does not use the whole page. It is colourless and there is an obvious expression of sadness. The upper part of the head is edged off the top of the page and the drawing is missing the body.

Because Rachel began this school session saying that she had been sick the night before and describing body symptoms which are reflected in the drawing, there is an obvious indication of her own deteriorating physical self. The edging on the upper part of the face could be part of that symptomatology or could reflect her wish not to think about what is happening. An encouraging part of the image is that the original neck was less than half the width of the one shown; the erasure resulted in a neck which would have an improved ability to support her head. Her story is as follows:

> Well she's crying because she just fell on the gravel and she scratched all up on her knee. She's also crying because her mother told her not to go out. She's always crying. She's also crying because the guys don't like her and also she's crying because her Mom promised to take her to Disneyland and she didn't.

When viewing this drawing and reading the story there is a profound sense of sadness, discouragement and hopelessness. The girl in the story has many reasons for crying, caused by both physical and psychological pain. 'She's always crying.' There is an allusion to Rachel grieving an unlived adolescence, 'The guys don't like her,' next to broken childhood dreams, 'her Mom promised to take her to Disneyland and she didn't'. Rachel had actually gone on a trip to Disneyland with her family and it had been a wonderful experience for her in spite of the illness. To think of the girl in the story being promised the trip and then denied it would be a severe deprivation in Rachel's mind.

The painful distortion of the face, the tears, and the bleak story suggest a growing awareness of a poor long-term prognosis. These combined with saying 'she's always crying', could support Bluebond-Langner's Stage 3 or 4 'Always ill' but we are not sure at this point in time of her view of her future. Is it 'will' or 'will never' 'get better'? Certainly, there is sufficient material around illness and deterioration to suggest this drawing could be placed in a category of Decathexis.

Medical records

On February 27, 1985, Rachel's haemoglobin was 10.3 grams, her white count was 3600, and her platelets were 60,000, all slightly improved. She had petechiae (small skin haemorrhages) under her chin, on her arms and on the back of her hands. She had a large bruise on her right elbow. Her doctor at that time reported that she was 'well in herself'.

Parent journal

No new entry.

Drawing 4 Drawn February 28, 1985, this picture's focal point is the central figure of the Rainbow Bright Google. He is looking off to the left, as were the wolf and the girl in previous drawings, again suggesting something cannot be faced directly. His right eye is smaller and his right leg is thinner than the other. His facial expression is not a smile, yet is not especially upset either. The Google's posture is rather indecisive or ambivalent. Although he is looking to the left, the placement of the arms and right foot suggest his body may be turning to the right. He is under the cloud, similar to the girl in the first drawing, only this time the cloud has three colours: yellow, blue and pink. The creature is called Rainbow Bright Google, and the cloud has a multicoloured rainbow image. The outline of the Google's body is suggestive of fluffy clouds in children's drawings.

The castle is edged on the right side of the page so that no door or access is visible to the viewer, and it appears to be floating. It has three levels, the third topped with a pyramid shape. There are three windows heavily framed with bright colours, the same as the cloud's three colours, and this is the only part of the drawing in which solid colour is used rather than just outline.

The viewer initially feels the cheerfulness of the bright colours and the hopefulness of the rainbow images. The addition of pink to the cloud could suggest being more 'in the pink' than the girl in Drawing 3. However, these positive feelings are somewhat dampened by the ambivalence and vulnerability of the Google, particularly after one reads of this one-year-old Google who is uncertain about where his home is:

> Once upon a time there was a Rainbow Bright Google. And he was wandering by the castle in the tall grass. And it was a beautiful day out like it was all the time. And he realized he was outside, 'cause he was only one year old. And it was a beautiful castle he was standing by. And he thought to himself, 'Is this my home?' And he went in and realized it was.

Trying to place this drawing according to Bluebond-Langner's model is difficult given the sequential nature of the model, but Stage 3 'Always ill and will get better' still seems appropriate.

The rainbow, a symbol of the connection between heaven and earth (Herder Symbol Dictionary 1986), is implied in the triple colours of the cloud and castle windows. The name Rainbow Bright Google as well as his shape suggest a merging of his symbolism with the cloud/rainbow. Thus, in spite of some uncertainty, the overall tone of this drawing is one of optimism, and in the joining of heaven and earth, one of Rebirth. Although he wanders under a cloud initially, the Google finds his new home in a beautiful place, inside the castle; it seems as if the unconsciousness realizes there is a home beyond this body.

Medical records

No new entry.

Parent journal

The family had consulted the hospital psychologist about Rachel's anger. He indicated how common it was for children to experience swearing as an effective outlet for anger and agreed with them in approving Rachel's request on March 3, 1985, for permission to swear, even using the potent 'F' word, in the privacy of the bathroom at home.

Drawing 5 This was created on March 6, 1985. The focal point of this drawing is the recreational vehicle, especially the bumper. It is the only brown part and is darker than much of the rest of the picture. Rachel's initial attempt at creating the camper was using white oil pastel, but once she saw it would not show clearly on this paper, she switched to light blue. The original shape was square with the front of the cab just barely reaching into the present cab's location. She re-drew the camper larger, rectangular and with the added length of the new cab, making it roomier. There is a small pink driver's window with a cross-piece in it, and two purple van windows with curtains which could suggest a domesticity or a decreasing view both in and out. The blue door has a large doorknob and the opening is above the steps and landing, making access a bit difficult. There is some confusion about the line at the top, whether it is the top of the van or blue and green mountains behind the van. There is a blue line across the top of the page for the first time, hinting that the heavens are now closer, but although it is out-of-doors, there is no sun.

The wheels are the oddity. They are made of a circle within a circle. There are four visible wheels, the middle two touching the van. There is a variation in the size of the wheels, and they should cause the van to point down into the ground if they were all attached to the vehicle or to direct it upward if a horizontal ground line were drawn along the base of the wheels. The trajectory of the van is off to the right, but with the present wheel arrangement, it would either be grounded or airborn before it could go far.

There is a feeling of optimism about this picture which is continued in the story:

> There was these people. They just retired and they felt like a little break. So they went out in the country where the wild life lived.

> And at night they sort of got a little scared, but not that scared because deer and fawns came up to their windows and the animals started to love them. And so they decided to live there. And they lived happily ever after.

There is a new phase of life for the people in the story who have retired or completed their work. The first night is a little frightening because they are now in an unknown area where the wild life lives, but the deer and fawns help them feel safe so they stay here and 'live happily ever after'. In a sense they see the animals first through the windows while still safe in their mobile home. The non-threatening nature of the deer and the love of the animals help her conscious self trust and be more comfortable with this unknown country. The images of travel, a new 'life' and the fawn, are all supportive of a Rebirth categorization. Because of the bright future, it would seem that Bluebond-Langner's Stage 3 'Always ill but will get better' would be the best of her placements for this drawing.

Medical records

A consultation from the attending physician on March 6, 1985, indicated Rachel 'has done quite well although she experienced nausea and vomiting that morning'. Further on, the concern of this caring doctor is expressed, 'I am still terribly afraid of this girl relapsing.'

Parent journal

No new entry.

Drawing 6 This drawing of a fierce gorilla was made March 12, 1985. The focal point is the cage. The text indicates there are strong bars, yet they are not attached to anything. They are so widely spaced in places that the gorilla could easily slip through. They form a barrier, but not an insurmountable one.

The gorilla presents some oddities. The face is very unclear and the features are out of alignment with the mouth facing front but the eyes off to the left. The position of the left leg and arm suggest it may be turning. The body is somewhat out of proportion, and part of the lower body and left arm are filled while the rest has much less colour to it.

The brightest colours are used on the filled-in images of the fruit and carrot. One could wonder if these might represent medications fed to control the disease, the fierce gorilla symbolizing a temporarily caged or controlled illness or even her own anger. If the gorilla were to look into the mirror in the cage would it see the reflection of the swing, suggesting perhaps the ups and downs of remissions and relapses?

The feelings evoked by this drawing include an unease about the gorilla and his ability to escape the barriers. His distorted face makes one confused and puzzled about what he cannot face clearly. There is also a strength or power about these colour images, yet the viewer is not certain whether the strength is with the disease, the child, or both. Her story was:

> One day a girl named Melody went to the zoo. And she saw a gorilla. And these people were feeding him oranges, apples, carrots and bananas. And there was even a mirror and a swing there. And there were strong bars. He looked fierce.

Although the fruit and carrot suggest vegetative, rebirth images common in dreams of dying adults (von Franz 1986), the bars, the fierce gorilla and overall tone suggest this is a Decathexis drawing. One has to be cautious in labelling this according to Bluebond-Langner's stages because there is some suggestion that the disease, if symbolized by the gorilla, is under some control for now. However, this control appears rather tenuous and may change quickly. Perhaps this drawing is from Stage 4, 'Always ill and will never get better'.

Medical records

No new entry.

Parent journal

No new entry.

Drawing 7 This picture was drawn March 14, 1985. The focal point is the huge picture in the art gallery. The 'punk' girl makes what looks like scribbles on the picture, although the text indicates 'they look like scribbles, but they are really eyes'. These are a series of yellow, orange, green and finally purple vertical and horizontal ovals. When the girl returns to the Art Gallery one of these 'eyes' winks. She thinks it is a trick, but the picture knows what she is thinking and replies, 'No one is tricking you.' When she asks, 'Who said that?' the picture replies, 'I did,' and the girl wakes up. There is both a trick and a dream in the text. The dominant image from the drawing is eyes upon eyes upon eyes. One wonders about being watched and about what the girl is seeing. These scribbles are not what they seem to be, they are eyes that know what she is thinking. They are framed in a dark purple, a colour associated with 'control or a need to have others support and control. It may indicate that one has a cross to bear' (Bach 1969). Given that the punk girl's face and hair are also purple, one must consider the importance of the colour.

The girl is oddly drawn. There are four sets of repeated eyes in the picture on the wall, yet one has difficulty seeing the facial features of the girl. She has disproportionately large black legs and huge feet but no arms or hands. She is a very small figure under this large picture. The story for the drawing was:

> There was an art gallery and this punky girl made a design on the picture. It looked like scribbles, but it wasn't. It was eyes. It looked like scribbles, but it was actually eyes. One day she came in to the gallery and one of the eyes winked at her. Then she thought, 'Somebody's tricking me.' Then the picture said, 'Nobody's tricking you.' She looked around. 'Who said that?' Then the picture said, 'I did.' Then she woke up.

The feeling tone of this picture and story is one of depression, anger, confusion, and turmoil. One wonders what is going on, for things are not as they appear and may be a trick or a dream. There is a foreboding about this drawing. Because there is an uncertainty about the future (the girl simply 'wakes up'), placement in Bluebond-Langner's Stage 4 is appropriate. The multiple colours hint at rebirth imagery, but the dominant images are the depression and helplessness of the girl in the presence of the huge picture looming over her. Therefore, this drawing can be categorized as Decathexis.

Medical records

On March 18, 1985, Rachel's haemoglobin was 10.7, her white blood count was 7800, and her platelets were 190,000, all much better. She was started on a three-day course of ARA-C subcutaneous, and again the doctor's note stated that she was 'well in herself'.

Parent journal

No new entry.

Drawing 8 In this picture created March 27, 1985, the focal point is the series of windows. There are six in total: one on the main floor which is boarded over in brown, two on the second floor – one with a cross in the middle but no ghost and one without the cross but with the ghost – and three on the third floor, the central one boarded over and the two outside ones each containing both a ghost and a cross. Rachel said that these ghosts did not have eyes because ghosts can see without them.

The oddity is the decay of the house. Although it is drawn in March, the image is more typical of a child's Hallowe'en drawing. According to Rachel, there are 'white, really bright blue, black and brown patches', yet the lower left is strangely empty or devoid of colour. The base of the house is very uneven and the door is well above this base. The doorknob is disproportionately large. Her story is as follows:

> Once upon a time there was this girl named Suzanne. It was night time. Suzanne was walking. She had run away and she saw this house. It was a patchy house. It has white, really bright blue, and had black and brown patches on it. She thought, 'I think it's empty. No one lives in it. I think I'll live there for a while.' She went in and saw this creaky stairway. She went up, creak, creeak, creeeak, creaak. And a ghost looked around the corner and said, 'There's a trespasser in the house.' But this was just a trick. But she didn't know that. So she went to sleep. The ghost came and scared her and she woke up and screamed. She saw a hole in the roof. She jumped as high as she could and just caught the edge of the hole and pushed herself up. And there she saw her lost brother. He had ran away years before.
>
> The End.

While she is escaping, this runaway girl sees a brother, 'lost' years before when he too ran away. Yet, although there is a reunion, there is no 'happily ever after' or any other suggestion of future. The ghost in the house knew she was there and tricked her. She wakes up, screams and runs, her only escape being through the roof.

The symbolism in this drawing is rather complex. There are three ghosts who seem to have intuitive vision; there are three crosses suggestive of the suffering of the crucifixion. There is trickery and running away; and there is a decaying house or residence. These combine to give the viewer a feeling of fear and foreboding. The large black areas make one wonder about fear, repression, and prognosis. Even running away does not help, there is no way to cover up or block this progressive deterioration and when the girl tries to avoid it, the ghost or spirit awakens and frightens her with the real situation – that her body, as symbolized by the empty house, is dying. This drawing can be classed as Stage 4 and as Decathexis.

Medical records

A test of the cerebrospinal fluid indicated that abnormal cells were present in large numbers. The blood work indicated all the counts were down which was not encouraging.

Parent journal

On March 28, 1985, Rachel said, 'Mommy, children are closer to God than adults.' Rachel often spent time alone in her room and then would come out and just state these rather profound thoughts, not giving anyone time to respond,

> She just gave me the most beautiful, gentle smile and turned and went back into her bedroom . . . She only gets irritable when she is tired now . . . after she had played hard, and play hard that child has done since she has had leukemia . . . she would put three hours into twenty minutes.

On April 2, 1985, her mother wrote, 'I just realized coming home from the hospital that she isn't going to get any better than she is now.' Her journal continued by mentioning an increased number of hospital visits and the necessary medical procedures.

Drawing 9 This drawing was made on April 10, 1985. The bridge across the top is one focal point. It appears to consist of twenty-four segments, although in reality only nine are completely divided top to bottom. The bridge almost spans the page, stopping just short of the upper left edge. This yellow-brown bridge drawn in outline separates the solid blue of the sky from that of the waterfall.

The oddity in the drawing is the four black rocks. They started much smaller, but as Rachel chatted while she drew, they were made larger and larger. Somatically, one wonders if this could reflect cells in the spinal fluid, as the bridge is also suggestive of a spinal column and the waterfall, of fluid. With the exception of a very small area on the left, their large size still does not divert the flow of water. They would however pose a danger to the man in the story:

> Once there was a man. He went down in a barrel. And he woke up from his dream and he got into a barrel and did the same thing as in his dreams. He broke a leg. He woke up in the hospital. He wondered what happened. And he lived on.

As she drew, Rachel said it was a waterfall and mentioned a news story of a man who had gone over Niagara Falls in a barrel. The text indicates that a man 'went down in a barrel'. He awakens and wonders what happened, but then does in real life what he did in his dream. He wakes up in hospital with a broken leg and 'lives on'. There is now a very clear representation of the future, and this way of phrasing it is unusual in children's stories. Also unusual for Rachel is that the drawing has no representation of the main events described in the story which accompanies it.

The symbolism of the bridge could suggest a joining of two different places, left to right, except that the poorly attached left side could collapse with any weight on it. The bridge as a barrier between sky and water is there but it is not very strong. In fact, there is a single vertical, blue line joining the two in the upper left, implying a union of conscious and unconscious. The waterfall could suggest a sudden, swift and powerful change of direction in the course of life, yet the flow of water, or life, is still strong. The dangerous rocks are there as potential obstacles, but have no apparent effect on the water or the barrel.

These ambivalent images generate a feeling of uncertainty and confusion in the viewer. There is an unease about the precarious situation here. Again, there is a dream and an awakening to reality, this time of an overtly described broken body. One wonders about the repetition of the injured leg. While the bright colours and the water image suggest hopefulness, the intense black of the rocks, the questionable bridge, and certainly the content of the story create feelings which mirror the abrupt downward movement of the waterfall. This drawing can be categorized as Stage 4 'Always ill and will never get better', and as Decathexis.

Medical records

On April 1, 1985, Rachel's lumbar puncture results showed many unusual cells. Her peripheral blood results were all grossly abnormal. On April 9, 1985, they were worse still, haemoglobin was 8.8, white blood count was 2200 and platelets were 6800, and the spinal puncture indicated the abnormal cells had gone from 82 per cent to 86 per cent. On April 16, 1985, the doctor mentioned four courses of intrathecal Methotrexate, and that ARA-C and 6MP (mercapdopurine) would be started. Rachel made regular trips to the hospital as an out-patient for treatments. She had 'prolonged marrow aplasia,' which means her marrow had been depressed for an extended time. She was unwell with a chronic disease which would alternate between remission and exacerbation.

On May 10, 1985, she was admitted to Emergency with severe bone pain, especially in the right femur (her upper leg). She was pale and cooperative. By May 15, 1985, her blood work had improved, but was still grossly abnormal. A doctor's consultation written May 15, 1985, indicated she was experiencing bone pain in her arms and legs and also intermittently in her abdomen.

Parent journal

At this time, Rachel got her first bike which 'changed her whole attitude about the outside world because it was her first bike . . . and she lived on her bike'.

Relatives from out of town visited over the holidays and Rachel again mentioned that children are closer to God. When asked how she knew, she said, 'Because [they] haven't been here as long.' Her mother wrote that Rachel would just state a thought or what she thought was a fact, and . . . that was the end of it. She left us sort of hanging there all the time:

> Now through this period of time Rachel was adjusting very well . . . She was actually feeling better. All this talk about dying, heaven and everything would stop even in the evening . . . I think this was the beginning of acceptance because she was getting more and more at peace. It was when she wasn't feeling good that she was vulnerable and that was when it would really come out.

By April 25, 1985, Rachel was having frequent, severe headaches. On May 3, 1985, her mother wrote, 'I know her count has dropped because she's pale and tired . . . can't help wondering if the medication may not be working and the cells are again invading her spine.'

In early June, 1985, her mother wrote that Rachel had come stomping up the stairs, looking frustrated, upset and close to tears. When her mother asked her to explain, she replied, 'Mommy, I know things, I can't explain why I know these things but no one taught me, not you or Daddy or my teacher. I just know things.' As they talked, her mother realized that Rachel had 'contact with a wisdom far greater than ours'. One of the doctors had commented that Rachel was eight going on forty, for they had seen this maturity also.

Drawing 10 Titled 'The Rabbit Disguise', this drawing was created on June 3, 1985. The focal point is the large rabbit. It appears to be turning to the left, yet it looks out of the page at the viewer. The tiny x's up the front of the rabbit's body are the zipper, for this is a costume, 'The Rabbit Disgoise [sic]'. Although Rachel had asked for the correct spelling of disguise, she printed it this way. The rabbit is not grounded and almost seems as if it is floating.

There are many things which make this a significant picture. First, it has been drawn vertically, which is not the usual position for Rachel's pictures or for most children's. It is the only one drawn in pen. It is the first to have Rachel's printing on the front, to have a title, to have flocks of birds in the sky and to have the sun on the left. There is considerable pressure showing on the back of the drawing; almost all of the large rabbit and the small rabbit with feet, all three words in the title, the bottom-right bird and upper bird among the clouds are all created with noticeable pressure.

The word 'rabbit' is central in the drawing, reinforcing the importance of the image. The usual symbol of rabbit is one of fertility, rebirth and resurrection such as with the Easter Rabbit. Here, however, the large rabbit is not genuine, it is a man in disguise. He has put on another appearance. As the big rabbit he frightens away the little ones, reminiscent of the earlier wolf frightening the children:

The Rabbit Disguise

> Once there was a man and he loved carrots. And he was looking for work. And he spotted a store with a rabbit suit. So he bought the rabbit suit. And he loved carrots – you have to remember that! He lived in a cabin in the forest. There was only one carrot in that whole forest that every rabbit was trying to get to. Now this rabbit suit was very large, bigger than all the other rabbits. And when he got to that carrot all these other rabbits began coming. When they saw him they scadoodeled! And he ate the carrot.

This man, disguised as a rabbit and living in the forest, finds the only carrot in the whole forest, even though they all have been seeking it. We are told in the text that, 'He loved carrots – you have to remember that!' It is interesting to note that this colourless carrot is in the same placement as the bright orange one in the gorilla's cage drawn previously. The viewer is left wondering what the carrot might symbolize to this child on one level and on an archetypal level what the story may symbolize. The ego or consciousness, symbolized here by the man, moves into the unconscious as represented by the forest. He first decided to buy a rabbit suit and by wearing it is able to find what he loves, the carrot. By symbolically choosing to move to the animal level of the unconscious, represented by putting on the rabbit suit, he is then able to access a deeper level still, the vegetative or primal level as represented by the carrot, an underground plant root. While the man eats the carrot or internalizes a basic truth of life which would include certain death of the body, this knowledge is frightening to the smaller rabbits, just as the conscious knowledge of her fate is frightening to this child.

All of the significant aspects of this drawing and text combined with Rachel's comment, 'I used to draw good rabbits, but I don't now. I've changed,' plus the fact that her best friend had just died of leukaemia make the viewer realize that an important change has occurred. With a jolt of reality, the viewer feels the sadness of loss, both for the friend and for this child. There is bleakness, almost a despair which joins with a fear of what is happening.

By putting on a new appearance, the man/rabbit gets his carrot. The little rabbits are frightened. The sun has moved to the west and birds, often representative of the soul, transcendence and flight to heaven (Cooper 1978) appear. Rachel seems to have moved into Bluebond-Langner's Stage 5 'Dying'. The symbolism suggests that this is a Decathexis picture.

Medical records

June 12, 1985, Rachel's haemoglobin was nearly normal although her white count and platelets were still slightly depressed.

Parent journal

> Rachel has gone through being very frightened and is scared too . . . I saw the pain and the tears and the loss on her face when [her friend] died . . . disease just does not attack the physical part of the child, it also attacks the psychological and it really plays havoc with the children because it unbalances them . . . and so the turmoil was just terrible for her.

Drawing 11 Titled 'The Flower Bed', this was drawn June 5, 1985. The focal point is the tulip on the right. It began with a shape similar to the two other flowers, but Rachel erased it and re-drew this one. The four points on the tulip remind the viewer of wholeness, totality and completion (Cooper 1978). The flower is formed by nine concentric tulips encasing an inverted bell shape. As she was drawing it, Rachel was talking about her friend's funeral. The back of the page reveals a great deal of pressure on the whole tulip flower and its leaves. There is also considerable pressure on the letter 'f' in flower, on the sun's nose, on the 'X' in the centre of the left flower and its stem, and on the left leaf of the middle flower.

The oddity is the left flower. It has four concentric lines forming the blossom compared to five for the central flower and there is a large 'X' in its centre, the only time in the series this happens, and the line for the stem, if extended, would join with the 'l' at the end of Rachel's name. This could symbolize the recent death of her friend or awareness of her own death.

Rachel announced that she wanted to do the drawing in pencil. There was much erasing of the flower on the right, as her friend's funeral was discussed. She said all the flowers were different, and identified the one on the right as a tulip when it was finished. There are three flowers and three flocks of birds. She volunteered that the birds were [as she pointed left to right] 'crows', 'robins', and 'eagles', then changed her mind and identified the middle ones as 'hawks', not 'robins' [crows, hawks, eagles]. The sun on the left is very large and there is no colour in the drawing.

Although the symbolism of birds, sunshine and flowers could be considered rebirth images in some circumstances, in this context the colourless drawing is more indicative of Decathexis. The flower bed could also suggest flowers on a grave, a custom with which Rachel was familiar. The huge sun could wilt these flowers, and the one on the left has been X-ed out in its centre. Two of Rachel's friends had died of leukaemia, one a few months before and one a few days before. Perhaps the three flowers represent the three children, with Rachel now recognizing what her own prognosis is. There are three flocks of birds in the sky but the initial robins, symbolic of death and resurrection, were changed to hawks. Now all the birds are associated with solar images and the ability and power to soar heavenward.

On viewing this, one experiences a sadness and a sense of bleakness, the reality of death as a grim prospect is clear. According to Bluebond-Langner, this would indicate Rachel's awareness that she is dying.

Medical records

No new entry.

Parent journal

No new entry.

Drawing 12 Created June 6, 1985, this was titled 'The Sad Monster'. The focal point is the monster. He approaches from the left and is outlined in purple with filled-in green legs. Rachel described him this way, 'He's got lots of hair, one eye, and three legs. He's sad. He wants to be buddies.' Although he is a monster, he does not appear especially frightening to the viewer. As Rachel drew him, wrote the title and coloured in the legs, she was speaking about funerals and about remembering.

There are two oddities, the monster's limbs and the stick figures' replies. Only two limbs are coloured in solidly, and the third is attached directly to a 'leg'. There are three limbs on the monster with three digits on each one. In response to the monster's statement, 'I want to be buddies,' three of the tiny people say 'Yes', but one says 'No'. Psychologically, this could indicate that the monstrous knowledge of her own death, coming from the unconscious is now on more solid footing, although one part of her still denies her fate. The heavy, solid purple of the hair on the monster's head and back may suggest a need to repress or contain this knowledge somewhat.

If he continues in the direction he is going, the trajectory suggests the monster could trample the little people. Does befriending the monster and letting it come closer mean annihilation? The green base of this drawing began as 'hills in the distance' but were covered over with brown as Rachel spoke about funerals and friendships. Her best friend's funeral was that day, and she said, 'Who wants to see a coffin' and talked about why we have funerals. The green/brown of the picture's base being coloured while funerals and burial practices were discussed suggests it could be grave symbolism.

There is a gentle sadness about this drawing, both from what we are told about the monster and also from the responses of the people. A separation is implied by three of the four agreeing to be buddies with this monster. One wonders who is left out now and what the monster may symbolize. Perhaps it is death and the little people or children are the three leukaemic friends. That could suggest that at a conscious level Rachel still denies her physical fate or perhaps one quadrant still struggles with the outcome of her leukaemia.

Although there is an offer of friendship and colour has returned, especially the bright green which suggests new growth, there is still the huge, overwhelming size of the monster compared to the people, the discussion during the drawing and Rachel's real life events to indicate that this is again a Stage 5 drawing. Although there is some rebirth imagery, the dominant feeling is one of Decathexis.

Medical records

No new entry.

Parent journal

No new entry.

Drawing 13 This picture was created on June 10, 1985. It is a complex image. The flowers quickly attract attention; there are four of them in four separate pots. Three of the pots, outlined in blue, appear to bounce off the top of the cart and the stems on those three flowers do not reach their pots when they are coloured with felt tip pens. Only one pot is secure and that flower's stem reaches right into it. This pot is shaded, not just outlined. This image is reminiscent of the four little people in the previous drawing – three are in one group and the fourth is different. There are also three sets of three concentric circles on the cart. The two outermost circles in each set are pink with pink dots or tiny circles in the spaces between them, and the centre of each is blue.

There are three oddities in this drawing. The first one is the flower on the right which has nine sharply pointed petals. There is a great deal of pressure evident on the back of the drawing where these petals are. The centre of this flower is very darkly shaded, first with tiny pencil squiggles and then with orange felt tip pen covering them. It is the only flower in the series like this.

The tire is the second unusual aspect of the drawing. It was erased and re-drawn, but the flat part is still on the right side not on the bottom. Because the Chinese man pulling the cart is saying, 'Oh no, a flat tire,' the viewer knows what it should be like.

Finally, the man himself is also odd. He appears to be ungrounded and has no feet. He is very tiny compared to the cart if he is actually pulling it. In fact he may not be able to move it with such a size difference but if he could, his grip is poor, on one handle only. If he pulled from where he is standing, the direction of the cart would tend to change. The man's grip, size and grounding cause confusion about what the trajectory of the cart really is.

Symbols in this drawing include flowers, but the survival of three is in question. The flower cart has a flat tire, and the man's ability to move it or get a grip on it is in question. 'Three concentric circles signify past, present and future' (Cooper 1978, p. 36) and there are three sets of them in this drawing. Given the repetition of three in the recent drawings, it is again possible to wonder about Rachel's association of her disease with that of her two deceased friends. The drawing generates frustration and uncertainty. There is a sense of precarious balance, futility and helplessness. This is a Stage 5 'Dying' drawing and also one of Decathexis.

Medical records

On July 10, 1985, Rachel's haemoglobin was down slightly, her white count was up and now within normal limits, and her platelets were still slightly low. A consultation on July 12, 1985, indicated she was doing extremely well and felt physically well. By August 7, 1985, her blood work was abnormal again, the worst it had been in three months. She was on all three of the chemotherapy drugs again. On August 8, 1985, a spinal tap showed 79 per cent blast cells in the CSF. By September 5, 1985, this was up to 94 per cent, where there should be zero to two per cent at most. Her liver function tests indicated it was essentially normal. The report on September 9, 1985, indicated she had had 'another recurrence'. On September 13, 1985, the consultation indicated she had experienced ten or twelve headaches in the temple area which may have been side effects of the medication or caused by 'arachnoiditis', that is, an inflammation of the lining of the brain or spinal cord. [It is interesting to note that 'arachnida' is the Latin name for spider, the subject of one of her first drawings.] By September 17, 1985, the blast cells in the CSF were down to 5 per cent and she was given a blood transfusion. It continued for an hour and a half, then was slowed and finally discontinued because of a blood reaction: shivering, low temperature and fast pulse. On September 20, 1985, she had more blood work done, had a spinal tap and was given medication. The results indicated she was improved.

Parent journal

On August 13, 1985, Rachel came out of her room with tears in her eyes and told her mother she had heard angels' harps. Her mother went back with her and could only hear wind chimes and a ghetto blaster outside. Rachel was very indignant, saying she could hear those too, but she had also heard the harps. As they talked, Rachel expressed her fear that the angels were coming for her, and again her mother was able to reassure her, telling her the angels just wanted her to know she wasn't alone. Rachel replied, 'Next time I hear them I will stay and listen instead of running away.'

Again in the summer, as her mother was serving a plate of corn-on-the-cob, Rachel asked, 'Mommy, if I die what will happen to my face?' Some time later a book her mother read indicated that this is not an uncommon question. Another time Rachel asked what would happen to her toys. This was new behaviour, or symbolic language, because in the past she had been feeling vulnerable when these topics came up but now she was feeling well. Her mother suggested Rachel might want to write out what she wanted to have happen to the toys and put that in her secret drawer. That prompted a giggle and Rachel said, 'I sure don't want to be around if someone went into my secret drawer.' Her mother said Rachel 'did tell me her favourite teddy is to be with her in her coffin'. She also made certain her mother knew her favourite songs and her favourite flowers, pink roses. She was always very matter-of-fact when talking about these and her mother said, 'I believe she was telling me in her own round-about way "This is what I want".' Her mother also indicated that Rachel 'was already into the fourth and fifth stages [of Bluebond-Langner's model] in 1985 . . . into the fourth when it turned acute [in April]'.

On September 6, 1985, they were told the cancer cells were back and the treatments would have to start again. They were also advised to consider radiation treatment. On September 9, 1985, Rachel was having bad headaches and pain which responded to heat and Tylenol. On September 11, 1985, Rachel expressed her sadness for all the children suffering from the procedures and treatments, 'I feel so bad, Mommy, while I see them be sick because of their chemo.' Rachel was very loving at this time and did not seem 'as troubled or angry anymore'.

Drawing 14 This is one of the first drawings that Rachel made after school resumed in the fall, drawn September 23, 1985. The focal point is the large butterfly. It is huge compared to the trees and flowers. Judging from the intense pressure on the back of the antennae and facial features, the sensory aspects of it are emphasized, and the initial pencil outline of the body is also heavy. Although it would seem to be the butterfly's body, the size and solid black colour suggest a chrysalis also. The non-symmetrical wings are only outlined; the pattern on the left is made of sixteen dots, six in orange and ten in purple, with six in matched pairs, and on the right wing there are thirteen dots, nine orange and four purple with only one pair and one triplet. The face on this butterfly has either a big, toothy smile or an open apparently smiling mouth with clenched teeth.

Tree trunks create the oddity in this drawing. They were coloured with a light yellow, but then covered over with black. The usual selection of colours was available, so one wonders what this covering up could symbolize. Because none of the trees appear rooted, and in fact the bases tend to curl upwards, there is a suggestion that they are beginning to drift upwards. This allusion to lifting or floating is true for all the trees, flowers and butterflies. The three deciduous trees are still green.

Although the symbolism of flowers, green trees and butterflies could suggest Rebirth, there is a feeling of emptiness in the butterfly wings, and apprehension or unease from the lack of grounding and from the black tree trunks and insect bodies. The tension on the back of the drawing, combined with these concerns, suggests that the rebirth imagery is not dominant at this point in time, and that repression and fear are dominant. Therefore, the overall impact and tone of this drawing is one of Decathexis. Because Bluebond-Langner's final stage is dying, there will be no further reference to her classification of the drawings.

Medical records

On September 26, 1985, Rachel's CSF blast cells were down to 2 per cent, almost normal and her blood work was only slightly worse than the last report six days earlier.

Parent journal

No new entry.

Drawing 15 This abstract drawing, 'Time Machine', was made on October 3, 1985. One main focal point is the dark blue outer layer. Its inverted 'u'-shape is suggestive of a road and the black intermittent marks, of the dividing lines between the lanes of a highway. If one took this image further, it is suggestive of the road of life, in this case almost coming full circle just off the bottom of the page.

As one follows the multicoloured layers in this drawing, there is a suggestion of a rainbow. The whole image started out white, while Rachel was speaking of the Ice Tunnel at NBC studios in California where she had been with her family. As she described the sensations of being in the tunnel while it rotated, and spoke of her trip to Disneyland and other locations, she added colours. The vibrancy of the colours and shapes suggest a much greater energy than the frozen white beginning of this image.

When asked if the completed drawing had a title Rachel called it 'Time Machine' and then commented that you can go forward or backward, indicating that the two red dots were controls. She then volunteered, 'I've had a good life. I don't want to see the future.' Although that is a very powerful statement from a dying child, the feeling tone of this image is joyous, and vibrant. There is a sadness and a denial or resistance if one hears the words only, but with this image there is also a strong sense of Rebirth, or hopefulness which is also its classification.

The control buttons indicate you can go forwards or backwards so that the one operating the machine still has some form of internal control over what is happening. Bach (1966) suggests that white may signify life's completion when all other colours are used. Here, however, Rachel does the reverse, using quite a bit of white but then colouring over it with bright colours. Her usual bubbly affect at the time of creating this picture was only mildly subdued, even while describing her life. It is interesting to note the similarity of this drawing to two of the drawings analysed in case studies by Bach (1969, pp. xxi, xxv). In those, as in this drawing, the bright 'rainbow' image is the entire picture, using the full page. The inverted u-shape is pronounced and they are all drawn at times where physical well-being of the children is in danger, but psychologically the promise of peace is recognized.

Medical records

On October 5, 1985, Rachel had another lumbar puncture. Although the results of this procedure and the blood work on October 7, 1985, were not encouraging, both the medical staff and the family chose to delay treatment because Rachel was going to be a flower girl at her older sister's wedding. On October 9, 1985, Rachel took part in an occupational therapy art group. She painted three pictures with 'bright colours and varied symbols and shapes in combination'. The first 'was a combination of flower shapes and drops of paint which she then smudged'. The second was a 'portrait of her older sister who had accompanied her and who was painting as well, which she also smudged'. The third picture 'depicted a stormy day'. Rachel agreed to leave all three of them at the oncology clinic for display. 'She worked quickly and happily and appeared quite happy with her participation.' Her mood was 'light and positive in spite of the lumbar puncture following after which she quieted markedly'. Her physical examination was essentially normal although it was noted that Rachel reported 'shivering in the past while'. She was restarted on chemotherapy.

Parent journal

On October 7, 1985, her mother noted that Rachel was thin and not feeling well. They were concerned about her response to her older sister being married and leaving, but Rachel thoroughly enjoyed being flower girl and adjusted well. Later, her mother said of this time, 'sure she had accepted her death . . . she knew she would be going, but boy she was going to live as best she knew how right up until the end.' That night Rachel was taken to Emergency yelling 'somebody help me!' and sobbing because the bone pain in her legs was terrible. On October 17, 1985, a bone marrow aspiration and blood tests were done to see if Rachel was still in remission. The following morning they were told she had relapsed. In spite of the bad news, Rachel's mother continued to stress how gentle and supportive the doctors and staff were. She also commented that the subsequent dates slipped by so quickly that she tended to record only on a calendar from then on, and wrote very little in the journal. About this time Rachel's parents became very aware of her increasing turmoil of the impending separation,

> as the months went by and she finally accepted the inevitable, like immortality . . . and she came to be at peace with it . . . she had a terrible, terrible time . . . I think that the hardest part for her was to finally not only accept, but to say goodbye . . . I think it was one of the hardest struggles for her. She said, 'I don't want to leave you and Daddy,' and she would cry, she would just sob, terrible, terrible sobs . . . and that was the time that was very hard for her because she knew she had to separate from us.

Drawing 16 Titled, 'Beware of Ghost!' this was drawn on October 18, 1985. The focal point is the house. Written near the bottom right are the words 'NO EXIT'. Nearby are two doors, more suggestive of institutional doors than those of a home. There are three windows with crosses in them and with broken glass. The fourth window is a soul window – circular, with a cross in the middle and placed within one triangle of the roof. The house has a patchy appearance. The roof is split in the middle, divided into two distinct portions. This may allude to discussions of a subsequent surgical procedure where a chemotherapy reservoir was implanted in her brain.

The oddity is the number of arrows. The picket fence along the bottom, broken and falling over in places, reinforces the larger arrow image which is the left wing of the house. This oddity became evident to the author when the whole drawing was traced for study. Rachel outlined a dominant part of the house on the left side, creating the effect that from the base up to the roof it forms an arrow pointing skyward. This part of the drawing is also suggestive of a booster rocket with a space capsule on it. The triangular roof with the soul window shaded in pencil would be the part to separate and continue upward. The text accompanying this drawing indicates that this little portion of the house is nice and clean and that this is where the ghost lives. It is the only homey, safe image in the drawing. When the teacher asked 'Can you tell me about the picture,' Rachel pointed to different parts of the drawing and described the following:

> *Beware of Ghost!*
>
> The bird is looking at the house, 'I want to get outa here.' [The tree without leaves] 'I'm cold.' It never had any leaves. [The ghost, lower right] 'I'm going to get that bird and eat him.' [The fence] 'I hurt.' 'Cause it's all broken.
>
> The house has boards over the holes. It has broken windows. 'I'm scary.' The attic window's not broken. That's where the ghost lives. It's nice and clean there in that room.
>
> [The tree leaning towards the house] It's a covering tree. The mud puddles are there because there's just been a big, bad storm with thunder and lightning.
>
> [The moon] 'What a scary place! I don't even like to look at it!'

The barrier would once have been the fence, but it is so broken now that it could not protect the house. The house is the central image, and the other features almost form a circle or protective u-shape around it. The orange tree trunk is out of proportion because the part near the bottom is narrower than the section higher up, adding to the precarious nature of it. Most objects are only outlined, although some are coloured in with a pale orange or shaded with pencil. The effect is one of a problematic situation, lacking in colour or energy. Because it is well into October, this haunted house image is not out of season, but the symbols are very bleak: a fearful bird that wants to get away, a ghost in the bottom right that wants to eat the bird, a tree that is cold and never had any leaves, a 'No Exit' sign, a dilapidated house, and the signs of a recent storm. It is so frightening that even the moon does not want to look at it. These symbols combine to create an image of physical deterioration and departure of the soul or spirit from the body.

The feelings associated with this drawing are fear, danger, helplessness and hopelessness; most things are broken and vulnerable. Although there is also a small sense of protection and security from the 'covering tree' on the left of the house and in the nice attic where the ghost lives, the overall placement for this drawing is still Decathexis.

Medical records

Blood work was done on October 15 and 17, 1985, and a bone

marrow aspiration was performed on October 21, 1985. The conclusion was that Rachel was in relapse, and that she had acute lymphoblastic leukaemia (ALL). More blood work was done on the 24th and again on the 31st which indicated it was almost normal; the chemotherapy was effective. On October 31, 1985, she experienced more leg pain. She was admitted to Emergency with vomiting and fever on November 7, 1985. At that time, the CSF was clear and her blood work had improved. By November 9, 1985, her haemoglobin was normal but her white count and platelets were low.

Parent journal

No new entry.

Drawing 17 'Monster' was drawn November 12, 1985. The focal point of this picture is the monster itself. The dotted outline of the monster body is unique in the series. The blue of its body is the same as the blue of the sky, causing one to wonder if this is a heavenly creature. The arms are purple, but continue with the dotted style. Does this unique style suggest a fading in and out of life or perhaps an ambivalence? The eyes are a dark, solid purple and seem to be looking at the tiny person on the right of the page, towards which the monster body is leaning. This monster does not appear especially threatening, and is somewhat reminiscent of the Google drawn earlier. These shades of blue and purple were two of Rachel's favourite colours along with pink. The monster image appears to be rising or floating and is almost framed by the green ground and evergreen trees.

The oddity is the house. It appears to be below ground level at the base, at least half a floor down. Two windows are very darkly coloured in green and orange. The whole house is outlined in orange, which Bach (1969) indicates may suggest a life and death struggle. The roof is not aligned, the door is also out of alignment, and the doorknob is quite high, especially for the size of the figure upstairs.

The chimney is the same bright pink as the monster's navel, rather than red as commonly used by children (Thompson & Allan 1987). It is interesting to note that a chimney is commonly seen as a site of departure for the soul, and the navel is seen as symbolic of unity between the spiritual and earthly worlds. This causes one to ponder what similarity or symbolic connections they may represent at a conscious, and more importantly, at an unconscious level for this child. The tiny person in the upper window is calling 'help'. This may be directed to the monster asking for help or to anyone for help from the approaching monster.

When asked if she ever felt like that person, Rachel shared a great deal, but prefaced it with a request not to tell her parents because she did not want them to worry any more than they already were. It seemed that just then she, like the little person, needed help. If the crumbling house represented Rachel's physiological state, then she was not doing very well. If it represents the family, then from Rachel's perspective, the edging off the right of the page and the lack of access could suggest her protectiveness of them at the time.

There is fear and ambivalence, yet also some hopefulness in this drawing. There are two evergreens; each of them has nine branches. This may be symbolic of the nine years on her own tree of life. These evergreens suggest optimism. The use of pink on the chimney and navel implies hope for a future haven at least spiritually if not in her own body. The dual nature of the monster (friendly/dangerous) and the two colours of the house (green/orange, or healthy/dangerously ill) also suggest ambivalence. The dilapidated house, the call for help, the sun on the left and the smaller right window and right eye of the monster, however, all suggest Decathexis. There is both the physical failing and the implication of leaving this life for another.

Medical records

Blood work done on November 14, 1985, indicated the best results she had had in some time.

Parent journal

No new entry.

Drawing 18 Entitled 'The Baby Robin', this picture was drawn November 15, 1985. The focal point is the newly hatched robin. It is outlined in the bright blue usually reserved for the sky, and Rachel indicated she had seen it outside her window that morning, obviously making it out of season in November. It has a tuft of golden yellow hair in the centre of its head, bright blue eyes, and a prominent beak with two distinct nostrils. The bottom of the body is barely touching the nest, almost as if the robin is rising. It has the red-orange chest typical of 'robin red-breast' and two pink shapes which appear to be wings. Around the bird, there is a white colour which Rachel identified as the broken eggshell. There are brown lines flowing from the robin outward and upward, suggestive of extended wings.

These markings are the oddity, for that would make two sets of wings and without verbal clarification it would appear to be three sets. It is possible that these brown lines are not wings or that the smaller pink lines do not represent wings either. However it is very easy to perceive the brown, white and/or pink markings as precisely that, wings. It is interesting to note that seraphim and cherubim, the two highest orders of angels, are described as having more than two sets of wings (Herder 1986, Cooper 1978). One wonders what these colours really are and what having two or three sets of wings might be like.

Rachel used two shades of brown, two shades of yellow, two shades of blue as well as pink, red and white. She added the white shell last. The pink wings are somewhat filled in as is the red breast. The eyes and nostrils, sensory organs, are solidly filled in.

The symbolism of the robin is death and resurrection (Cooper 1978), and the egg represents resurrection and hope (Cooper 1978, Herder Symbol Dictionary 1986). These reinforce the image of new life implied by a baby bird and especially of this one which is rising up out of its nest. The emotions elicited by this drawing are joyous and hopeful. The feeling of being uplifted comes from this striking Rebirth imagery.

Medical records

No new entry.

Parent journal

No new entry.

Drawing 19 'Apple Core' was drawn on November 17, 1985. The focal point is the person's face, especially the eyes. The pupils are dark, looking down to the left at the apple core, and again the right eye is smaller. The nose has distinct nostrils, as did the robin in the previous drawing. There are freckles both on the person and on the sun, whereas Rachel usually drew them only on her suns. Also, both the person and the sun have toothy grins. Strong pressure is evident on the pupil of the left eye, on the figure's teeth and on the smile of the sun. In addition, there is extra pressure on two-thirds – twelve – of the sun's eighteen rays, those nearest the bottom.

The oddity in this picture is the missing body. There is a large head attached to two feet which are joined at the heels. Before she erased it, Rachel began the line for shoes much lower and larger on this page. If this drawing is overlayed by the baby robin (Drawing 18), both main images would have been of identical size before this one was erased. Now the person's head is about a quarter of an inch higher than the robin's and the body is about two inches further up from the bottom of the page. When overlapped, the change from the erasure suggests that this person is floating higher than the robin is.

The word 'Yum' appears on the drawing. The apple has been eaten and only the core is left. It has no seeds in it. The sun appears to be looking at the person; and the person to be looking at the apple core. The person's shoes are laced up through four circles on one side and five on the other. One has the feeling of bleakness, of enduring or gritting one's teeth and bearing it.

There is no colour in this drawing; there is no body on the person; and only the seedless core remains of the apple which has already been eaten. Symbolically, the apple can be seen to represent the Tree of Knowledge, the forbidden fruit and also the fall and death of humanity. The image could also be seen as suggesting that while this child's core or essential inner being is intact and observing, her physical self has really been consumed and cannot produce new life in the future. Although there is some rebirth imagery in the rising figure and the new knowledge or understanding represented by the eating of the apple, the Decathexis images of deterioration and distancing are more dominant.

Medical records

On November 15, 1985, she contacted gastroenteritis with a fever.

Blood work and a spinal puncture on November 19, 1985, indicated she was doing quite well. A bone marrow on November 20 indicated she was back in the chronic phase of the disease, and there were fewer than 5 per cent blast cells which was greatly reduced although she was not in remission. A new drug, K-asparaginase, was instituted at this time.

Parent journal

No new entry.

Drawing 20 Titled 'Land and Sea', this picture was drawn November 22, 1985. The focal point is the dark brown boat. The section of it behind the princess is higher than the other end. According to the story:

> The princess is being carried back to the king's castle [upper left] so she can TELL him she's going to marry the slave. Then they're going back to Castlegar to get married and go to Nelson to live.

Once she has journeyed by boat to the blue castle and spoken to the king, the princess with her bridegroom/slave will return to the towns in the upper right for the wedding ceremony and to live, the latter site being the town in which Rachel had lived prior to being diagnosed. The princess can see the castle and is prepared to face that part of her future telling them she is leaving, but perhaps the return 'home' is not yet something she is able to understand, hence a barrier in that direction.

Both people have eyes, but no mouths or noses. All of the figures' eyes are the same colour as their outline except that of the princess, her eye is very black. The bottom half of the page is taken up by shades of brown and gold. It is not clear if this is the sea bottom or the 'Land' referred to in the title. It could symbolically represent the depths of the unconscious from which her increasing awareness departs to 'tell' consciousness she will be leaving.

There are solid colours on the boat and oar, on the slave's head, and on the two towns in the upper right, the rest of the picture is outlined. The oddity is the transparency of the living images, the people and fish. The body of the princess does not touch the boat at all, and the slave's body only reaches it at one spot. The towns of the wedding ceremony and residence in the upper right are golden yellow and in the placement of the sun in earlier drawings. The blue water is at the top of the page where blue sky has been in the past. There are nine fish, all swimming to the right according to Rachel. Five of them are on the right side of the boat, 'behind' it, three are beside or in the shadow of the boat and the last one on the left looks as if it will collide with the boat. This could mirror her first five cancer-free years, three more fighting it and the last or ninth year ending abruptly.

There are many symbols in this drawing. The fish symbolism just described, and the direction of the boat – going to the left and opposite the school of fish – suggest death images. Dreams of travel to the west, to the setting sun, and in a boat are all common death images according to von Franz, and 'in my experience the image of the journey in dreams is also the most frequently occurring symbol of impending death' (von Franz 1986, p. 64). The princess is a helpless occupant of the boat as they go to tell the king she is leaving. Perhaps her dark eye is seeing that all the life is fading. Although the image in this picture evokes a feeling of serenity about the journey and a new life, there is a very clear message announcing her departure. While there is some Rebirth imagery, it is a Decathexis drawing.

Medical records

No new entry.

Parent journal

No new entry.

Drawing 21 'Bear in the Snow' was made December 4, 1985. The focal point is the snowman, especially the arms. The left arm is not attached to the body nor to the hand. The right hand appears to be in front of the broom and does not have a grip on it. The whole picture is done in pencil, outlined only except for the hat and triangular nose which are shaded. The snowman has three segments; the upper body was erased to move it to the right, and the head, to make it larger.

Most of the drawing time was spent erasing this bear named Fred 'to get him lighter' and this concern for faintness is the oddity. Fred is drawn in the central position; the broom is a barrier between him and the snowman. Both characters have the same vulnerable arms-outstretched posture. Fred's right eye is very small and only his right foot is touching the ground. He too is wearing a hat, but rather than shaded, the designs were erased repeatedly. The following story accompanies this drawing:

> Fred bear lives with his Mom and Dad in a warm, happy hut. He came out on a cloudy day to build a snowman.

The number six is repeated in objects: six coals on the snowman, six steps to the house and six segments on the chimney. The snowman's arms, hat, facial features and coals all have extra pressure on the back of the page, and so do the six steps, door, window, and six segments of the chimney. The lines on the sidewalk and chimney create an impression of movement flowing upward on the right.

The edging of the house causes one to wonder what could not be shown. There is much smoke coming out the chimney which may reflect a great deal of emotion in the family at this time (Thompson & Allan 1987). The cloudy day could also reflect overcast times. Both the snowman, who will melt, and faint Fred bear suggest a fading from life. The bear is a symbol of resurrection (Cooper 1978, Herder Symbol Dictionary 1986). The story indicates that Fred bear lives in a warm, happy hut with his family, suggesting security and love. There is however a feeling of melancholy, repression and evasion about this drawing. The warm, happy hut will be very hard to leave but the fading figures and cold day dominate the page, just as Rachel's disease dominates the cold reality of her future. This drawing is also one of Decathexis.

Medical records

No new entry.

Parent journal

> In February, 1985, Rachel had started complaining about being cold. She said to me, 'I feel cold, Mommy,' so I cuddled her more and she said, 'I don't mean that kind of cold . . . I feel cold all over and inside. I am cold . . . It is just a cold feeling and

> then it leaves.' Now my feeling about this is . . . when she got that cold feeling she was trying to come to grips with dying.

The feeling continued, and by November, her mother believed the cause had changed slightly.

> There is a separation. [Rachel] knows the separation. She could feel the separation. That is the coldness she was talking about. You know how terrifying that is. She knew it . . . I believe this . . . that she was already feeling the pull of it . . . the separation of the body.

Drawing 22 Called 'Rainbow of Light', this abstract drawing was created December 11, 1985. The focal point is the wide, yellow band of colour. Bach (1966) indicates this colour 'may suggest an emphasis of things of a spiritual or intuitive nature'. It is the same colour as Rachel used for hair on drawings identified with herself and the same one as on the curly head-feathers of the baby robin drawn previously.

The initial pencil lines show through this colour, emphasizing the impression of the colours flowing across the page. It is not clear whether the direction is downward towards the centre from the upper right or the reverse, flowing upward. There are eight bands of brilliant colour: on the right are pink, purple, and blue – all colours Rachel liked – and on the left of the central yellow band are two shades of blue and two shades of orange.

The emotion evoked by this picture is primarily joy, although the orange shades on the left elicit some mild unease. The rainbow is seen as a bridge between heaven and earth, as a hopeful, positive image. Children often include rainbows as part of a larger drawing, but it is more uncommon as the only image. Because the title is 'Rainbow of Light', the symbolism of light becomes important too. It includes the representation of God, spirit, and immortality (Cooper 1978, Herder Symbol Dictionary 1986). Images of light in various forms and of light-beings are common in the dreams of the dying, usually as very powerful, positive images (von Franz 1986). This drawing combines the two symbols, a rainbow and light, with brilliant colour to create a dramatic Rebirth image.

Medical records

Rachel was admitted to hospital on December 12, 1985 for surgery. Her examination revealed that she was in good health although a slight bruise was noted on the right inside of her mouth. Her height was at the fifth percentile and her weight between the thirty-fifth and fortieth percentile for her age. An Ommaya reservoir was surgically implanted in the right ventricle of her brain. The reservoir is another way of administering chemotherapy. The surgery went well, there was no facial weakness and no abnormal reflexes were recorded. A nurse's note of December 14, 1985, indicated Rachel was feeling faint. Her blood work on December 16, 1985, was near normal. The summary report on December 17 included the following comment, 'One year ago she developed acute blast cell transformation which responded well to the reintroduction of Prednisone' and the other drugs. 'Six weeks ago she was again in relapse.' The same three medications as administered previously were then reinstated. She was again in remission. Another part of the report indicated, 'She had always had CNS disease. Physical examination showed no enlarged liver, or spleen and no enlarged optic discs.' On January 3, 1986, the doctor mentioned two new drugs and commented, 'It is too early to tell if she will continue in remission.'

Parent journal

No new entry.

Drawing 23 On January 8, 1986, Rachel drew 'Fat and Little'. The eyes are the focal point. They are very detailed and large. There is an unusual amount of pressure on the back of the right eyelashes. One wonders what the little girl is seeing as she looks straight ahead with her eyes wide open. The oddity is also a facial feature, her huge smile. The teeth which appear in most of the other drawn smiles are missing in this picture. If they represent defence (Cooper 1978) and vitality and strength (Herder 1986), then one wonders about her physical state. What has changed? The outline of the smile is drawn with extra pressure.

The proportions of the figure are quite unbalanced. The head is huge compared to the body, taking up about three fourths of the page and, especially on the right, it is lopsided. The little body could not possibly support this size, and it appears that she is leaning as if she will topple over. The picture is outlined and has no colour. The upper body and right heel are also drawn with added pressure.

The distorted body image of a huge head and diminished body is reminiscent of the crying girl in Drawing 3. Here the body is shown as fat and little or powerless, but this girl is facing the situation, whereas the girl drawn earlier was looking down, depressed. That face was quite distorted; this one has very clear features, and even a smile. However, even though this girl does have a body, the proportion is distorted and there is a lot of tension around it. A common side effect of the drug Prednisone is an altered appearance or 'moon face'. This girl is also missing any ground to stand on and the outline of the head is faint, making this yet another floating/fading image.

The emotional response to this picture is one of sadness. Although one can see her facing the future with a smile and apparent brightness, one is also aware of her distress over her changing body, her sense of helplessness and her obvious physical deterioration. This is a Decathexis picture.

Medical records

No new entry.

Parent journal

No new entry.

Drawing 24 'The Ice Capades' was drawn January 9, 1986. The focal point is the character who has the word 'Snorks' on its costume. This figure is looking down at three columns protruding from an elliptical opening in the lower left. These upright cylindrical shapes are similar to the character's 'antenna' except that his antenna bends to the left. This character has large eyes for the size of its body and is the only one clearly on skates. However, with one foot apparently going in either direction, movement may be difficult. Because it has a costume on, the identity is unknown, another disguise. It has a star on the waist or belt. Von Franz writes that the star 'is another historically familiar symbol for the resurrection body' (von Franz 1986, p. 40).

Rachel's comments about the picture indicate that the characters had to skate over 'this great big hole in the middle' of the ice, yet this performer does not look frightened nor does the task seem especially dangerous or difficult. In fact the stance of this character suggests its trajectory would be in a circular pattern, either to the left or right around the hole.

One oddity in this drawing is the lack of faces on individuals in the crowd. Also, there are no extremities on the six faces nearest the ice, only concave body/necks, and it is unclear whether they are performers or audience. On each of the three figures who do appear to be performers, there is only a body, and again, no feet or hands. Another unusual feature is the two holes with three projections in each. They are not identified, and Rachel's only response to a request to describe the drawing was very vague in this respect:

> Well, that's me and my sister's boyfriend [upper centre]. He took me to the Ice Capades. They had on these costumes and they had to jump over this great big hole in the middle of the ice.

Ice is temporary and melts just as the earlier snowman would. It is also cold. The hole in the ice is a big spot right at the centre. Von Franz (1986) provides many examples of individuals who dream of black spots, some overhead, some as pits or holes which appear instead of the more common tunnel images in dreams of the dying.

For this drawing, the page is vertical and everything is outlined in pencil. There is no colour and the only shading is on the boyfriend's shirt. The figure identified as Rachel is distant and small, with a very indistinct face and body. Another interesting feature of this picture is the direction in which different characters are looking. The boyfriend appears to be looking off to the lower left and so does the 'Snork'. Four characters around the 'Snork' appear to be facing forward, but four others appear to be facing left. One wonders what is being seen both by the audience and by the performers.

In viewing this drawing one feels some alarm at the posture of the audience because they all have their arms above their heads. Is this excitement or surrender? One is uneasy about the lack of faces and of some bodies, and is uncertain about the significance of the hole at centre stage. There is a confusion as to whether or not characters are happy or just maintaining a pretence. Certainly, the great distance Rachel drew herself from the centre of activity suggests this is a picture of separation or Decathexis.

Medical records

No new entry.

Parent journal

No new entry.

Drawing 25 This picture of 'The Secret Garden' was drawn January 10, 1986. The girl is the focal point. Her posture attracts attention because it is an awkward way to stand and difficult to maintain. The left arm is barely attached to the body. The whole drawing is done in outline form, in pencil only. The girl's hair is shaded but Rachel did not fill in all the area she originally outlined which was the common style she used in pictures associated with herself. This represents a change. The face has a lopsided smile. The dress is united directly to the head, with no upper separation; and there are two heart-shaped buttons on the dress. This may suggest a greater unity of the heart and head.

The door is odd because it almost forms a frame around the girl, although her lower legs and feet are not included in it. The door is already covered with more ivy than the wall around it and Rachel's comment indicates that soon it will be very difficult to find the door at all. The doorknob is the other area that is heavily shaded and that shows a slight extra pressure on the back of the drawing. The wall forms a barrier separating this secret garden from the other side. The wall extends all the way to the right of the page although it is not as dark there and the ivy is not as thick. The two trees inside the garden reach from the ground up to a sky which appears overcast from above the girl all the way to the right edge of the drawing. The sun in the extreme upper left is not hidden however.

The three flowers and two deciduous trees in this garden are out of season in January. Although a garden suggests new growth, in the story of the same name as this drawing, which Rachel was reading with her mother, a child faces many difficulties including her mother's death and moving to a new country to live with an unknown uncle. The secret garden in that child's new home was a forbidden, secret place which had been kept sealed because a young woman fell from a tree and died there.

Now this girl in Rachel's drawing is in her own 'Secret Garden'. There are several images suggesting death: the sun on the left, the wall becoming a permanent barrier once the door is hidden, the vulnerable posture of the girl, and the two trees connecting the earth and sky. Although the vegetation suggests rebirth, it is overshadowed by these death images, by the overhanging clouds and by the lack of colour in the drawing. One feels a chaos and bleakness in the garden; there is a sense of pain, distortion, aloneness and separation. This is a Decathexis drawing.

Medical records

No new entry.

Parent journal

Rachel had spoken to her mother over this time and had indicated that she could hear God, but could not see him and asked about God's appearance. Another day, she came running out of her room excited and told her mother she knew what Heaven looked like. Her mother stopped cooking and said, 'You do?' She replied, 'Oh yes, I have been there before. It is beautiful, everything is so colourful there, the green colours are so clear, the trees and grass. It is because there is no pollution. Everything is so clear and bright.' Her mother's journal continues, 'I stood there stunned, then she gave me a beautiful smile and turned and went back into her room.' These comments from Rachel continued to surprise the family.

Drawing 26 Drawn January 13, 1986, this picture has no title or story. The central image of this brilliant abstract is the focal point. A light green, vaguely circular shape almost encloses a collection of bright solid circular and rectangular shapes. All the colours available were used, even white. Perhaps the two white dots represent two white cells, powerfully outnumbered by others now. The green outline almost forms a container and is suggestive of a mandala.

The balance of tensions or the equilibrium in this drawing is quite striking. The central image is held by matched images all the way around. There are purple lines at the centre top and bottom, orange u-shapes at the upper left and right, and red sections in the lower left and right with an orange heart in each. Lime green segments in the upper left and right each have a purple kidney shape with an orange dot in them. On either side solid bands of yellow, purple and green attach horizontal lines to the central image. On the central base are five lines radiating upward. The combination creates a balanced image, one of equal tension either pulling outward or pushing inward, or perhaps both.

Symbolically, these could represent the last equilibrium before the final dissolution of self begins. If these central colours are all aspects of the Self, then the lines could represent attachments to all things of this world. These attachments would include all those directed towards the outer world, and from the outer world holding onto the self. The central image is just beginning to break up at the bottom of the green enclosure. Bach writes, 'As the children have depicted in their paintings, at the end of their life's journeys psyche and soma may come together again before separating finally at a sychronistic moment' (Bach 1969, p. 64). Based primarily on her work with dreams of the dying, von Franz also writes of a final centring of the soul at the moment of death. If taken as a whole, this drawing projects a sense of balance, completeness and organization. The viewer experiences a sense of fullness or as Rachel would say, it is 'joyful', and obviously a picture of Rebirth.

Medical records

No new entry.

Parent journal

No new entry.

Drawing 27 'My Squiggle' was drawn January 14, 1986, and is the last of the series drawn at home. There is no one isolated focal point as the brilliant colours take up the entire page. Again, all the colours, including white, are used. Rachel began the drawing with a gently flowing or mildly twisting light yellow colour used in the Rainbow of Light. She added more and more colours in lines suggestive of the tight vibrations of an elastic band as it recoils from tension. Most of these are vertical or diagonal on the page.

There is a variety of blue, purple and red geometric shapes in the centre. There is a small, dark blue shape in the lower centre, suggestive of a crumpled, discarded form. The bright orange shape on the left of the page is suggestive of a crucifix. Von Franz describes the symbolism of the cross in Christianity as 'complete endurance of the conflict between violent emotions and their spiritual meaning' (von Franz 1986, p. 119).

This drawing could be seen as a vibrant, chaotic and energetic representation of dissolution of the Self. It seems as if the central dots and the fine balance of the last drawing have snapped and now all is in a state of disorganization. Some lines suggest an upward flow but there is no clear pattern at all. This is a Decathexis drawing.

Medical records

On January 15, 1986, Rachel was taken to the Emergency Department with a high fever (40.4 degrees Celsius), diarrhoea and a stomach ache. By January 19, 1986, her temperature was down to 36.9 degrees. She was mobile although she was suffering from an oral lesion. Later, she was up and playing and a nurse noted she had a 'very mature attitude toward her illness'.

Parent journal

'I knew on the night of the 14th [of January, 1986] that she was in serious trouble. I sensed things yet she kept up a bright, cheerful attitude.' She told the family, 'I am not coming home. I am going to die soon.'

Drawing 28 'Zig Zag' was drawn in hospital on January 18, 1986. Rachel sat cross-legged on her bed and cheerfully created this final image. It contains broad, strong bands of colour: two greens, two blues, red, orange, and the yellow of the Rainbow of

Light. Although not shaped like a rainbow, this drawing contains all the colours of one. White, brown and black are not used at all. The gently flowing lines overlap. The two shades of green are in shapes suggestive of fish and the lighter green one is the most intense. This drawing evokes feelings of harmony, strength and peacefulness. It is a powerful statement of the peace Rachel achieved.

Medical records

On January 22, 1986, Rachel had petechiae on her cheeks, ears and chest. Over the next week she was mobile and socializing in spite of increasing bone pain and abdominal discomfort, bleeding from various small sites, frequent nausea, extension of the petechiae and a rash. In the early morning of January 30, 1986, Rachel experienced generalized seizures lasting ten to fifteen minutes which were then localized to the right side with right hemipelegia. She was transferred to the Intensive Care Unit. Despite prolonged efforts at resuscitation, she expired later that evening, January 30, 1986.

Parent journal

Rachel was nine years old when she died. Her funeral was February 4, 1986.

Drawing 1
Girl with spiders

Drawing 2
Hide-and-go-seek

Drawing 3
Crying girl

Drawing 4
Rainbow Bright Google

Drawing 5
Recreational vehicle

Drawing 6
Caged gorilla

Drawing 7
Art gallery

Drawing 8
Patchy house

Drawing 9
Waterfall

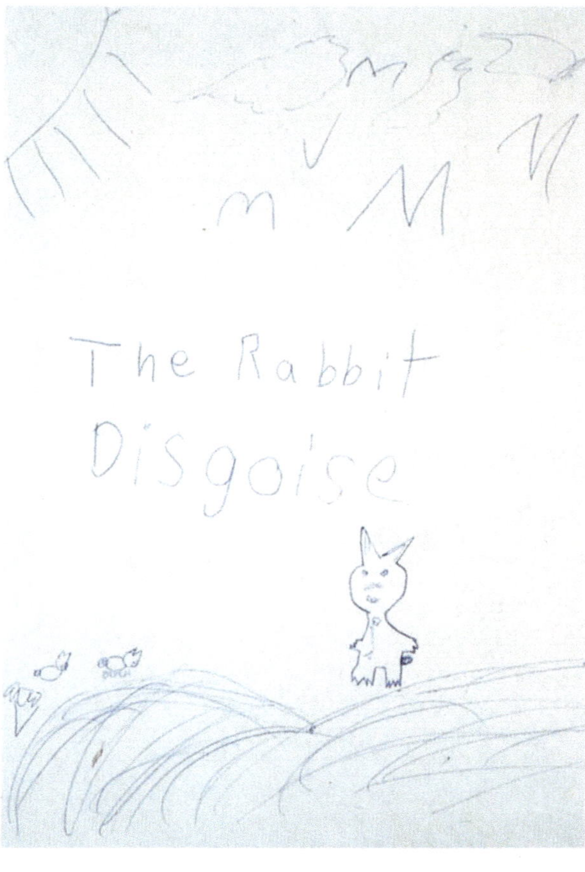

Drawing 10
'The Rabbit Disguise'

Drawing 11
'The Flower Bed'

Drawing 12
'The Sad Monster'

Drawing 13
Flat tire

Drawing 14
Butterflies with floating trees

Drawing 15
'Time Machine'

Drawing 16
'Beware of Ghost!'

Drawing 17
'Monster'

Drawing 18
'The Baby Robin'

Drawing 19
'Apple Core'

Drawing 20
'Land and Sea'

Drawing 21
'Bear in the Snow'

Drawing 22
'Rainbow of Light'

Drawing 23
'Fat and Little'

Drawing 24
'The Ice Capades'

Drawing 25
'The Secret Garden'

Drawing 26
Mandala

Drawing 27
'My Squiggle'

Drawing 28
'Zig Zag'

Drawing 29
'The Scout's Honour'

Drawing 30
'Heart to Heart'

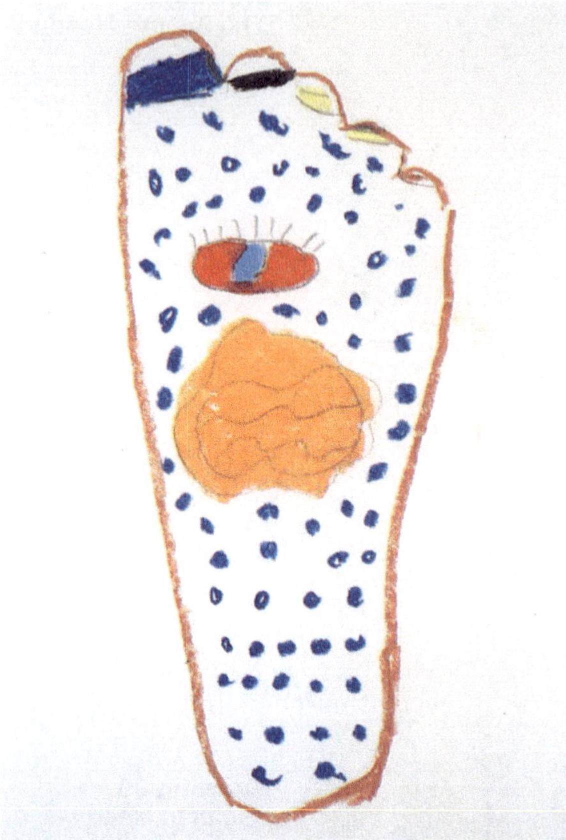

Drawing 31
Magic breathing holes

Drawing 32
Rosebush

Drawing 33
'Not Feeling Bad'

Drawing 34
'The Chinese Boat
on the High Seas'

Drawing 35
Sunset

Drawing 36
The robin and the worm

Chapter 5

What we learned

Reading Rachel's material provides one with at least a small sense of just how intensely moving her experience was, the violent chaos of dying somewhat balanced by spiritual serenity and insight. At this point it is helpful to summarize the findings from the detailed analysis. Patterns did emerge through the consistent use of specific questions and some issues were raised through the convergent material. Exploring these patterns and concerns make it possible to arrive at some conclusions about the themes in this material, thus developing a sense of having learned from Rachel's experience.

Picture analysis

Each drawing was studied at length using the pre-determined questions as analytical tools.

Focal points Although the focal point which first attracts attention in a drawing may vary from one observer to another, there will always be some aspect of the picture which pulls the viewer into the psychic content of the material. Working with that part of the picture is the beginning of the pathway for explaining the drawing, for becoming part of it, and so for understanding some deeply meaningful symbolism from within the creation. For example, in Drawing 7, at an art gallery, one focal point is the picture of eyes above a punk girl. One could pose the question, 'What would it be like to be this huge, all-knowing picture on the wall?' The girl's graffiti on the picture looks like scribbles but is really eyes, suggesting that some aspect of the girl (Rachel) has given the picture this chaotic yet all-seeing vision, and it now looms over her with a heavy burden, the knowledge of her death still contained in a purple frame. 'Why do I wink at the little girl below?' is another possible question for this focal point. The meaning behind a wink in Western culture can be a confirmation of being friendly or of sharing information not commonly known. This wink can be seen as a way of softening the ultimate knowledge of death, a private communication from the picture in the art gallery sharing the secret understanding that 'Nobody's tricking you'.

Another example, the bumper on the recreational vehicle in Drawing 5, could suggest questions such as, 'Am I a buffer for things left behind, or do I need to cushion the vehicle [self] from something that is catching up to me too quickly?' The bumper's solid lines and rich brown colour suggest a healthy purpose, that it is valuable to the vehicle which is moving forward into a new life even though that future is unseen by the back bumper. Questions such as these move the observer further inside the drawing, permitting insights and often stimulating still more questions.

Edging The most commonly edged features were the houses, usually off the right side of the page. In one case, the girl in the drawing was also edged off the top. Because edging suggests a need to deny or hide something from consciousness, these examples would indicate times when Rachel needed to protect an aspect of herself from the ultimate knowledge of her condition. This could be a protection from thinking about the disease or from experiencing overwhelming emotions. Since a house is also commonly seen as representing family, the edging may reflect her wish to protect them as well.

Pressure Pressure on the back of the page was evident in several drawings, indicating where the main physical energy had been focused during the drawing. This in turn indicates where the main psychic energy went. An example would be contained in Drawing 11, 'The Flower Bed'. The tulip was drawn with deeper lines, or more energy, both in the outlining and in the shading. Rachel was speaking about her friend's death and funeral as she worked on these. Obviously the physical intensity reflected the conscious sense of loss of her friend, but also indicates her developing awareness of loss of her own physical self.

Colour A total of twenty pictures were in colour and eight were done in black and white, one of these being done in pen rather than pencil. Two of the eight colourless pictures were drawn as Rachel appeared to move into Stage 5 'Dying' and three more appeared in a row in January just before her death. These three pencil drawings were her last pictures of concrete objects. There was no clear pattern in the use of specific colours, although a light yellow which may indicate a precarious life situation (Furth 1988) was often used for coloured hair. Rachel also associated this colour with her own blonde hair. Light blue, which may indicate fading away or withdrawing (Furth 1988), was the most common colour used for some part of the central image, such as legs on the first girl, the outline of the camper, and the baby robin's body. However, there was no clearly prominent colour pattern used throughout this series.

Outlining A trend noted by Furth (1973) was that leukaemic children tend not to fill in their drawings. Rachel also left much of each drawing in outline form, but she nearly always filled in some portion such as the hair on the first girl, the window frame on the Google's castle, and the gorilla's fruit. Many of her drawings also have sketchy lines filling in more objects such as the sweater dress, the wolf, and the grass. However, Rachel's abstract drawings generally have more solid forms. Perhaps these variations reflect the more precarious nature of her concrete physical self, the letting go of her outer world while also indicating the strong, solid nature of her more abstract inner being.

Setting Furth (1973) also noted that leukaemic children tended not to draw suns or outdoor pictures. In contrast, Rachel drew eighteen outdoor pictures, although only seven had suns. In his study, only healthy children drew suns with faces, but in this series two suns do have faces. While Rachel's drawings show some similarity to the trends noted by Furth, the variations could be explained by the progress of the disease and by the length of time over which it was possible to collect the drawings – three months in his study versus twelve months for Rachel's. Furth also noted that although there were trends the findings were not statistically significant.

In his study, Furth indicated that leukaemic children tended to place suns in the upper right quadrant. All of Rachel's suns prior to Drawing 10, 'The Rabbit Disguise', do appear in the upper right but afterwards, they all appear in the upper left. This shift in the placement of the sun may indicate a new, conscious awareness of her prognosis. Prior to 'The Rabbit Disguise' she was not fully aware of her approaching death at a conscious level, but once she moved to Stage 5 'Dying', her suns are placed in the left or west.

Abstracts Of the twenty-eight drawings in this set, twenty-three were of concrete objects, although two of these, the waterfall, and the art gallery could be viewed as partially abstract until the accompanying text was read. Five drawings were clearly abstract: 'Time Machine', 'Rainbow of Light', and the last three in the series. All of these were drawn in the last four months of her life. Furth writes, 'An abstract portion of a drawing or a whole abstract drawing usually represents either something that is hard to understand, difficult or obtuse, or an avoidance' (Furth 1988, p. 82). Rachel did not consciously understand her prognosis at the time of drawing the partially abstract art gallery and waterfall, and her stories from those months reflect a need to deny or avoid. The picture of the time machine was even accompanied by an obvious wish to avoid, 'I don't want to see the future.' However, the other four clearly abstract drawings in this series are more likely examples of difficult concepts for a child to grasp.

Text The text was very important for clarifying some drawings, especially for the future, with phrases such as 'lived happily ever after' or 'he lived on', guiding the viewer into the appropriate frame of reference for that drawing. While the future seemed to be indicated primarily by the wording of the text accompanying the drawing initially in this series, in subsequent drawings, fading figures in some form provided these clues. After Rachel reached Stage 5, the amount of text diminished greatly but the number of titles given for drawings increased markedly. This change can be partly explained by her diminishing physical energy as well as by an easing of requirements from her teacher. However, it may also reflect a telegraph approach to the content, a conservation of psychic energy condensing the verbal message to a more cryptic form.

Distortions and deterioration Distortions of faces and bodies such as in Drawing 3 of the crying girl and deterioration of houses such as seen in 'Beware of Ghost!' reflected the physical and emotional effects of disease, the impending death, and view of self. Crumbling houses like the one in 'Monster' and body distortion such as in 'Fat and Little' clearly reflect an image of the deterioration of the physical 'house' or self. Broken windows and distorted faces in the early drawings may indicate her difficulty with facing or seeing the fate which is shown so clearly later on in the series when whole parts of the body are missing.

Symbolic themes Potential danger such as the wolf and frightening images such as the fierce gorilla indicated threats to her well-being. In the first ten drawings and stories the frequency of tricks and dreams is quite striking. These reflect a form of denial providing her with defences against the knowledge of her death. Finally, some common symbols were noted: (a) placing the sun on the left, representing the west, (b) drawing rainbow images suggestive of hope and rebirth and (c) using traditional symbols such as travel and light, common in dreams of the dying.

Adult records The material from the parent journal supported findings from the in-depth analysis of the drawings. Rachel's attitudes, concerns, and health as reflected in the drawn images corresponded to the material her mother had recorded. The dreams and fears of spiders, the sensation of being cold, and the anxiety about separation and being alone are all examples of concerns which were recorded in both formats. The approximate timing of placement in Bluebond-Langner's stages also matched quite closely. Rachel's mother indicated that the family believed Rachel was moving from Stage 3 into Stage 4 during her anger phase which started in February, 1985. The wording of their thinking about Rachel's illness even matched this model at one stage as shown by her mother's comment, 'I just realized that she isn't going to get any better than she is now,' recorded in April of 1985. The drawings had indicated in March that Rachel was in Stage 4, 'Always ill and will never get better'.

The medical records, however, were much less supportive. There were cycles of remission and relapse which matched in a general way, but specific dates sometimes preceded and sometimes followed the image which suggested a change in her condition. The indications of a right-sided weakness, evident as early as the first two drawings, did not appear in the medical records until the day she died, and even then there was a right hemipelegia, not hemiparesis. Specific physical information was suggested some of the time however. For example, in Drawing 9, of the waterfall, the black rocks in the water hint at the blast cells in her spinal fluid, and the repeated leg injury in that story pre-dates the severe leg pain Rachel experienced a month later.

Classifications The process of classification was difficult. One major challenge in using Bluebond-Langner's model is that she bases her stages on a sociocultural perspective, saying it is 'possible to measure their awareness by examining their behaviour' (Bluebond-Langner, 1978, p. 234) especially in the context of interactions with others. In the material presented in this book, the assumption of awareness and subsequent assignment to a specific stage was based primarily on reviewing drawing content and only then considering information about behaviour. While some of the information available about Rachel matched closely with Bluebond-Langner's observations, such as her saying, 'I'm not coming home this time. I'm dying,' just as the hospitalized children said, some of the other behaviours Bluebond-Langner observed, especially the preoccupation with time and the almost nonexistent reference to any form of life following biological death, were very unlike Rachel. In the classifications presented here, it does seem possible to fit the drawings to the model, but only when drawings were seen as a group and had other supplementary material available; because the difference between Stage 3 and Stage 4 is based on how the future will unfold, either 'will' or 'will never' 'get better', the drawings in isolation could not clearly distinguish these stages. Those drawings placed in Stage 5 'Dying', however, were much easier to identify because of the imagery alone. Also, Rachel's experience conformed with the model's need to have a peer die of a similar disease after the child under consideration had reached Stage 4.

Classification into the categories of Decathexis and Rebirth posed difficulties primarily because aspects of both appeared in many drawings. For example, the most difficult drawing for the author to classify was Drawing 14, of the two butterflies and floating vegetation, because the logical analysis of content clearly suggested rebirth imagery, yet the emotional impact of the black, solid butterfly bodies made Decathexis 'feel' appropriate. Only after many days of indecision was the final placement resolved. That the author chose Decathexis so many times perhaps reflects personal material also. This author taught her alone, daily for a year and a half of schooling. It is quite possible that the selection of 'Decathexis' for so many drawings is a reflection of a continued sense of loss.

The other confusion with the classification is a questionable delineation of just where 'separation' ends and 'rebirth' imagery begins. The symbolism of a journey to a new home is an example of where this confusion could exist. There is a very subjective aspect to the human experience of endings and beginnings, of losses and new opportunities.

Jung states

> Beginning and end are unavoidable aspects of all processes. Yet on closer examination it is extremely difficult to see where one process ends and another begins, since events and processes, beginnings and endings, merge into each other and form, strictly speaking, an indivisible continuum. We divide the processes from one another for the sake of discrimination and understanding knowing full well that at bottom every division is arbitrary and conventional. This procedure in no way infringes the continuum of the world process, for 'beginning' and 'end' are primarily necessities of conscious cognition.
>
> (Jung 1960, p. 412)

This duality is further explained in relationship to death by von Franz who writes

> that the unconscious psyche pays very little attention to the abrupt end of bodily life and behaves as if the psychic life of the individual, that is, the individuation process, will simply continue. In this connection, however, there are also dreams which symbolically indicate the end of bodily life and the explicit continuation of psychic life after death. The unconscious 'believes' quite obviously in a life after death.
>
> (von Franz 1986, p. viii)

It must be understood then, that a single drawing may contain images recognizing the end of physical existence as well as expressions of belief in an afterlife.

Comments and queries

The doctor assisting with the medical records raised two concerns. First, the most troublesome aspect of the Bluebond-Langner model for this physician was that all children reach Stage 5 'Dying', and that they did so specifically after hearing of the death of another child. The mechanisms of how children in rural areas or even the first on the ward to die in some time could have heard about that other death was not something we were able to find in the source material. Therefore, although her model is based on her personal observations of forty leukaemic children in a metropolitan hospital, Bluebond-Langner may not have addressed this specific question. It seems quite evident in Kübler-Ross' work, however, that some children do know they are dying without seeing others die first.

Secondly, the doctor assisting with this study expressed some surprise at the rigid sequential nature of her model. In addition to those concerns, the physician was disappointed to understand how frequently the children in Bluebond-Langner's study had to resort to peers as a source of information, and indicated hopefulness that it was primarily a function of that hospital and not as big a problem elsewhere. The author then described an experience she had had with Rachel. After reading Bluebond-Langner's book, she asked Rachel about children having a secret place in the hospital for sharing medical information, and Rachel did confirm that there was a similar network here. She also indicated, however, that her own experience with staff and parents was different. Procedures, treatment options and side effects were discussed with her.

The final point raised by the doctor related to the physiological revelation in the drawings, such as whether Rachel drew freckles which could represent petecheiae. Drawing 19 included freckles on both the character and on the sun and medical records indicate Rachel did have petecheiae at that time. The use of patient drawings as indicators of physiological information had definitely not been a part of medical training, although some physicians are currently developing skills in this area.

Rachel's parents believed the Bluebond-Langner model was appropriate for many of the children they came to know in hospital. They also believed it was applicable for Rachel, but that in her case it did not fit as well because she was expressing death awareness much earlier than this model would suggest was possible, particularly when she was feeling vulnerable, that is, when there was a medical crisis. In discussing this phenomena with Rachel's family, the writer realized their consistent explanation was that Rachel seemed to be spiritually advanced. Although they always allowed her to express whatever she wanted to, they were not especially religious in a formal sense, and her frequent spiritual insight left them with a feeling of awe and puzzlement.

Rachel also did not seem restricted towards the end of her life to the anger and withdrawal apparent in the children in Bluebond-Langer's research.

Content themes

Numbers Several themes emerged throughout this series of Rachel's drawings. First was the repeated appearance of a series of numbers. Bach (1969) often found significance in repeated numbers as units of time in the child's life. In these drawings the repetition of nine could be seen as relating to Rachel's life span because she died at age nine. There were nine trees in the second drawing (Drawing 2), five plain ones and four with children hiding from the wolf, and there were nine fish in the drawing with the princess (Drawing 20), five swimming ahead freely, and four further behind. These could be seen as representing Rachel's five disease-free years and four more coping with the leukaemia. Each of the trees in the dotted 'Monster' drawing had nine branches, suggesting her tree of life.

The number three also might have been significant, for there were three ghosts and three crosses in the windows of the patchy house in Drawing 8. These may be related to repeated numbers in Drawings 10 to 13 made just after another friend died. In 'The Rabbit Disguise', there were three rabbits; in Drawing 11, 'The Flower Bed', there were three flowers and three flocks of birds; in Drawing 12 three little people said 'Yes' to the sad monster; and in Drawing 13 there were three sets of three concentric circles on the flower cart. The same three flowers from the flower bed appeared again in 'The Secret Garden' near the end of her life. It is possible to wonder if the repetition of threes represent the two deceased friends plus the recognition that Rachel too would die from leukaemia.

Another repetition over time was the appearance of a single

carrot in two drawings in this series, one brightly coloured in the gorilla's cage and the other one which the man/rabbit searched for and found in the 'Rabbit Disguise' drawing. It was interesting to note that each carrot appeared in the first drawing which had been assigned to a new stage in Bluebond-Langner's model. Although Bach (1975) frequently noted significant numbers in a child's drawing prior to knowing any history, caution must be used when fitting numbers to a case study, especially when much is already known about the history.

Images of a girl The most frequent image in the series was that of a girl. It appeared in some form nine times throughout the series. In the first drawing she appeared to smile, but the story indicated she ran home screaming because of the spiders others had put on her. In the second drawing she and other children were hiding from the wolf. Rachel identified herself in the first story and then used her initials in the second one. In the third drawing only the face and neck of the girl appeared. The girl did not appear in the picture for Drawing 6, but the story indicated that she was looking at the gorilla. There was a girl's image again in Drawing 7 at the art gallery, and her face was badly distorted. In Drawing 8 the girl who had run away was written about but not drawn. There was no further reference to a girl until Drawing 20 where she appeared as a princess. There was a series, Drawings 23, 24 and 25 with a girl shown, each in some way identified with Rachel, either by appearance or by having done that activity. In all of these drawings the girl was in some way distorted or vulnerable to unpleasantness. In some of these, the girl's face was unclear or almost off the facial area. The stories supported this theme of the girl being vulnerable, facing frightening situations or becoming distant.

These images reflect the young protagonist's constant struggle to 'face' her ultimate end. She is not given the foreknowledge of a mythical set of tasks to complete as were Persephone or Psyche, yet she relentlessly endures one challenge after another. She must confront the Great Weaver as represented by spiders, see fierce creatures, and come to know her own ghostly or intuitive knowledge – all within the first half of the series. She then becomes the princess carried away before maturity to be joined or married only at another, distant place across the water. The rainbow of light shows the strength of her hope for a new life, one beyond the distorted body she inhabits and which seems to be less and less complete. The final three images of girls confirm the end of the physical self as a girl changed by disease and separated from this life.

Monsters and predators Monsters and predators in some form also appeared frequently throughout this series. The monsters were not clearly frightening characters however. The first was the Google, only a year old and rather benign looking. The Sad Monster was huge, but really just wanted to be buddies with the little people, and the dotted monster in Drawing 17, also huge, was not clearly dangerous either.

The wolf, however, in Drawing 2 frightened the children. The gorilla too was fierce. The multiple eyes at the art gallery and the ghost hiding in the patchy house both frightened the girls in those respective stories. The man in the rabbit suit sought the single carrot as did the other rabbits. The hawks and eagles in 'The Flower Bed' were certainly predators. Even the title cautioned of the need to 'Beware of Ghost!' in Drawing 16, and the person in 'Apple Core' had consumed the fruit. These images can be seen to represent the fearsome, destructive nature of the disease, impending death and knowledge of separation. Yet, for the most part these images do not evoke terror; it is almost as if death can be friendly, although still monstrous, if one has an appropriate view of it.

Trickery Another theme which indicated Rachel's apprehension is that of trickery, dreaming and hiding which occurred in the first ten drawings. The first trick was when other young people put spiders all over her in Drawing 1. The very next drawing was of children hiding from the danger of the wolf. The eyes in Drawing 7 were tricking the girl and then she woke up. The ghost in Drawing 8 was also tricking that girl and she too woke up. The man in Drawing 9 also awoke, first from a dream and then in hospital, after going over Niagara Falls in a barrel. In Drawing 10 there was a disguise where the man hid who he really was. At this point Rachel's friend had just died and it appears that Rachel clearly knew she too would die. It was at this time that she started telling her mother about her 'favourites', music and flowers, which her mother believed was Rachel's way of helping to plan her own funeral. She also began asking what would happen to her toys when she died. Even though she knew unconsciously what was going to happen, she was only eight years old then and her defences provided her with a time of denial. Jung (1960, p. 405) states, 'Whenever possible our consciousness refuses to accommodate itself to this undeniable truth,' that the end of living is dying. This period permitted Rachel opportunities for a softening or buffering of the finality of her physical ending and for a strengthening of her belief that there is a continuation in an afterlife.

Fading and floating There was also a shift in Rachel's drawings from solid objects to fading and floating images over this series. Although Drawing 3 of the crying girl's head was only a partial figure, it clearly reflected the physical experience which Rachel explained had happened the night before and which she drew intentionally. However, beginning with Drawing 10, there were birds in the sky in some drawings. The rabbits and carrot were not grounded, nor was the flower cart in Drawing 13. None of the figures in Drawing 14 were grounded. The dotted monster in Drawing 18 appeared to be floating, and in the next drawing the baby robin was barely touching its nest. The person in 'Apple Core' appeared to be floating and the body was gone. Most of the images in 'Land and Sea' were transparent and Fred bear was just barely visible. His snowman would melt as would the ice in 'The Ice Capades'. The girl's body in 'Fat and Little' was almost gone. It seemed as if Rachel had fully understood that she would die at the point where the tricks and dreams stopped and had moved on to this theme of images which more clearly suggest distancing from this world, fading away physically and floating free of earthly attachments.

Intuition A brief but important theme was the sense of intuition which appeared early on in the series. In the first drawing, the girl knew to look in the bushes for people, even though she did not know they were there. In the second drawing 'they were scared [of the wolf] and ran away and it scared him [the wolf] too'. 'It' frightened the wolf away, but there was no indication of what 'it' was, only that something frightened him away. The young Google 'realized' he was outside and then 'realized' that the castle was his home. The eyes of the art gallery 'knew' what the girl was thinking. Finally, the ghosts in the patchy house could see without eyes. In the last two examples, the eyes seemed to represent intuitive vision, carrying on the theme of knowing purely through intuition. Rachel's intuitive or unconscious self already knew the outcome of her disease, just as months before she had said she would die, but most of what this intuitive knowledge shared frightened her and felt like a trick or bad dream.

Eyes Throughout the series, however, eyes on figures were also important for indicating whether the figures were facing the situation directly, by looking straight out of the page, whether they were avoiding it, by being distorted or looking away, or whether they were fixing attention on a certain character within the drawing. The eyes in many drawings were very large, almost cartoon-like and even suns had this type of eyes. The wink of an eye in the art gallery story suggested secret communications.

Eyes were significant on many levels then. First they indicated what Rachel was actually seeing through one of her sensory organs. Changes were happening to others on the ward and changes happening to her own body were clearly visible to her externally. These are represented in her drawings as deteriorating images along with the impact they created emotionally. At times the physical indications were too difficult to 'face' head on and so she drew images reflecting this inner distress. Sometimes the too large eyes indicate she may have 'seen' more than was comfortable. The sun in Drawing 11 looks down over a flower bed drawn as a friend's funeral was discussed and a new personal awareness was being reached. The figure in Drawing 19 looks down at a seedless apple core – the fruit eaten, no seeds left for new growth in the traditional patterns of life-cycle renewal.

Home One aspect of houses that appeared as a theme in Rachel's drawing was poor physical condition and edging of some buildings. The patchy house and the haunted house with no exit both had ghosts living in them and both seemed abandoned and crumbling. While the ghosts or spirits do not seem disturbed by the physical deterioration of their residences, for their existence is not in question, the ego is very aware that its end is at serious risk as the body succumbs. The Google's castle, and the houses in Drawings 17 and 21 were all partly off the page, as if something could not be seen or acknowledged at the time of these drawings.

Journey Another theme related to home was that of having, or travelling to, a new home. The Google realized the castle was his home, but at first was uncertain, as were the retired couple who travelled to where the wild life lived but then settled there happily ever after. The gorilla had a home in captivity, not in the wild. The patchy house was home to a ghost and a temporary residence for the girl who had run away. The man 'travelled' over the falls and as a result had a temporary place in the hospital. The ghost had a nice, clean room in 'Beware of Ghost!'. The princess was going home to the castle to tell the king she would be leaving for a new home, and Fred bear left his warm hut to build his snowman. Finally, in the story of the secret garden the child had to travel a great distance to a new home and in Rachel's drawing with this name the door out of the garden would soon become very difficult to find. All of these could be seen as representing the deterioration of her physical being, the temporary nature of her life and the anticipation of leaving for a new place of existence.

These references to a new home also reflect the classic human journey. At first one realizes that one has a 'home', complete with all that is associated with it. In Rachel's drawings the intense, colourful windows of the Google's castle suggest the love, hope and strength of home. As with the archetypal journey, this series reveals trials, pain and fear away from home once Rachel's journey has begun. Just as the gorilla had been captured and placed in the zoo, Rachel had been captured by the disease and forced on this journey. Yet, although given no choice initially, she is ultimately able to take some small control as represented by the princess telling the king she is leaving. This is reinforced in stories where she chooses to move from one place to another. In a sense she rehearses her final departure. One of Rachel's final drawings clearly indicates an acknowledgement of her death. The girl in that drawing has gone into the secret garden and the doorway will soon be obscured and inaccessible; once she is in the garden, there is no returning.

Transformation A final theme reflected within the content analysis is one of symbols representing optimism, hope, or transformation. The butterfly signifies transformation because of the changes within its life cycle. In Drawing 18 the black body of each butterfly suggests a chrysalis. Wings appear to be lifting the creatures, yet they are mostly transparent, just an outline of what they will become. These suggest metamorphosis, that Rachel was nearly ready to leave her earthly state for a celestial one. Babies, the Google, and the robin just hatched from its egg also suggest new beginnings. In Christian symbolism the robin signifies death and resurrection and the egg represents resurrection, re-creation and hope.

Another dramatic example of hope is the rainbow image. The rainbow was suggested in the clouds in Drawings 1 and 4 and was part of the name of 'Rainbow Bright Google'. A rainbow was suggested in the use of colour in 'Time Machine'. It was vividly evident in 'Rainbow of Light', and more subtle in the flowing harmony of the very last drawing. As a symbol of the connection between heaven and earth, the rainbow indicates an awareness of an ending in one form and the bridging over to another frame of existence.

The rainbow and the visible spectrum of light, seen in combination in the 'Rainbow of Light' drawing, is consistent with the findings of von Franz who also writes

> The image of light appears more often than any other image in our quoted material. Jung has expressed the assumption that psychic reality might lie on a supraluminous level of frequency, that is, it could exceed the speed of light. 'Light' in this case, would appropriately enough be the last transitional phenomenon of the process of becoming unobservable, before the psyche fully 'irrealizes' the body, as Jung puts it, and its first appearance after it incarnates itself in the space-time continuum by shifting its energy to a lower gear.
>
> (von Franz 1986, p. 146)

Rachel's rainbows, then, reflect a sense of hope and hint at an awareness of leaving the known, sensory world, moving toward light.

Emotional themes

Fear Emotional themes in the series began with fear. Those drawings with tricks and threats in some form such as the danger from the wolf and the 'bad trick' of spiders placed on her indicate an emotional response of fear. The feeling was either stated as fright or screams in the story, for example, as it was in the first two drawings, or it was suggested by dark colouring and size differences within the drawing as it was in the patchy house and the art gallery drawings.

Sadness Sadness was reflected in a similar manner, either by a clear description in the story or title such as in 'The Sad Monster' or by a lack of colour in the drawings such as with 'The Rabbit Disguise' and 'Bear in the Snow'. Extreme sadness and depression were suggested in drawings such as the third one with a girl who was described as 'always crying'.

Anger Very little clear anger was evident in these drawings, even at the time Rachel was overtly expressing anger in her behaviour with her family. One drawn example would be the punk girl at the art gallery, where her appearance and behaviour suggest she may have been feeling angry and rebellious, but it quickly turned to fear. Although there was pressure on the back of the page in many drawings, it would seem to have been caused from tension more clearly related to anxiety and emotions other than anger. An example would be the extreme pressure on the back of 'The Rabbit Disguise' which occurred when Rachel was speaking of her friend's death as she drew.

Emotional contradiction Some pictures suggested an emotional contradiction, such as the smiling girls in Drawings 1 and 23 which were accompanied by stories or titles which could cause the viewer to anticipate distress. This was also true for pictures where the sun was smiling, yet the circumstances at the time were very sad. Perhaps these reflect Rachel's wish to appear cheerful, or her deeper ambivalence about leaving family yet at times feeling comfortable with her concepts of an afterlife.

Facial expressions There was a sense of tolerance or resolution in many drawings throughout the series, often represented by a neutral facial expression no matter what the circumstances were. The Google realizing the castle was his home, Fred bear having completed his snowman, and the girl standing in the secret garden would all be examples of this resigned attitude. Many drawings suggested acceptance, happiness and even joy, either because of the smile on the main figure such as the one in 'Apple Core' and the implied smile as on the baby robin, or even because the image and story actually describe the happiness, as in the case of the retired couple in Drawing 5. Some of the abstract images suggested this contentment simply by the colours and shapes used; an example is Rachel's final drawing.

Implications for theory

Based on the in-depth and thematic analysis, it seems that the drawings of this child indicate she experienced alternating views of herself as physically deteriorating and having to separate from this world with views of existence in some form beyond that of her dying body. The convergent material from the parents could also be seen to support this view. The stages defined by Bluebond-Langner are supported by the drawings provided they are taken as a group and include any accompanying texts. Based on Rachel's experience, as revealed in her drawings, it is possible to explain a changing awareness of impending death using both models.

Prior to any of the drawings being made Rachel already appeared to have had an underlying, unconscious spiritual or intuitive awareness of death which she could partly articulate yet not really understand. This would correspond to the awareness described by Kübler-Ross, Bach and others. It appeared at first in statements made to family members. Initially, Rachel would say, 'I could die you know,' yet months later, 'I didn't know I could die from leukaemia,' or she would state a wish to go to Heaven so she could come back healthy. These examples both reflect typical childlike thinking of death, especially as being reversible. Over time, this awareness appears to have become a bit clearer to her and as it did, she reflected more congruency between the spiritual understanding and her childlike awareness which she was expressing verbally. As she moved closer to making conscious sense of her illness, she created drawings which appeared to reflect that inner spiritual awareness but only her stories could tell what she was thinking – that this was all a trick or a nasty dream and that someday she would get better. It would seem possible that the drawing reflected the inner unconscious awareness and that the story reflected where she was in her more verbal, conscious understanding. Also, as Rachel advanced through Bluebond-Langer's stages, there would have been an ending to, or death of, one view of self and the development of a new view; a death/rebirth pattern would reflect the progression through each of these five stages.

As Bluebond-Langner described the stages, the children believed one could be very sick yet eventually recover fully (Stage 3) but disease experience and knowledge, the elements which forced progression, moved Rachel into Stage 4 in March, 1985. She remained there until the death of a friend in June of that year forced her into a clear, thinking awareness and understanding. It would seem that once the spiritual part of her was reconciled with the cognitive child operating in the world, once she reached Bluebond-Langner's Stage 5, once both conscious and unconscious self knew and could articulate that she, too, would die, then she could move forward into dealing with her leave-taking. She could begin giving directions to her mother for her funeral; she could address the pain, and the cold, empty feeling of leaving her family behind. This could account for the changes in her drawings and the text after June, 1985.

This combination of models explaining both the spiritual and cognitive aspects of her awareness could also account for her family's confusion about why she did not match Bluebond-Langner's model exactly when she first began speaking about her own dying. If this spiritual knowledge precedes cognitive understanding, it could also explain how some of the children described by Kübler-Ross and others seemed to know on their own, intuitively and without contact with other terminally ill children that they would die. Kübler-Ross noted that for some children this awareness was, in her terms, 'preconscious' or not clearly understood by the child. Bluebond-Langner's model, while accurately reflecting the behaviour and statements of those children in hospital, was based on their outer world and intellectual process, and did not include the inner, spiritual concepts. These spiritual concepts would appear to be ahead of the child's existing, conscious awareness which organizes and understands the world based on logical experience and cognitive development. In this case study it was only when both the spiritual and the intellectual aspects of the child were in harmony that full understanding truly reached her. This occurred in June 1985 when she had integrated her friend's death with her own knowledge, experience and intuitive understanding.

Only then was she also able to continue working towards a spiritual acceptance and the development of some comfort for what would happen afterwards. Her unconscious self seemed to prepare her, 'not for a definite end but for a profound transformation and for a kind of continuation of the life process which, however, is unimaginable to everyday consciousness' (von Franz 1986, p. 156). These preparations were expressed in a child's language and within a religious context because these were available to her and were part of how she made sense of her world. Perhaps the increase in the number of abstract drawings she made in the last four months reflects the difficulty that the spiritual part of her had in explaining those complicated concepts. The reality of one's own transformation and continuation beyond biological death is very difficult to grasp even for an adult, whether using language or any other traditional image of humanity.

Rachel's experience as reflected in the drawings would seem to indicate that on an intuitive-spiritual level she knew very early on what would happen to her. From the beginning, the drawings show death/separation images interspersed with those of rebirth, and the number of rebirth images increased slightly towards her last months. On a conscious level she had to progress slowly with her understanding, resistance and tolerance. However, as death moved inexorably closer she reached an integration of the two levels, working through many attempts to deny the outcome. These defences are reflected in the drawings from Stage 3 to Stage 5 made between February 1985, and June, 1985. Once she could no longer deny her prognosis at any level, it seems she continued to work at tolerating her pain-riddled experience emotionally and physically. As this tolerance for the inevitable grew, she also gained spiritual insights to both her physical end and to what was beyond. Although the latter was not expressed in any clearly understandable form for those who remain to read her material, there is a profound sense of hope in her legacy.

Chapter 6

Suggestions for helpful interactions

Many children who have faced life-threatening illnesses have provided insights about their daily contacts with other people. They value certain styles of communication and interaction with others throughout their illness and often find specific expressive strategies to be effective tools for coping. This final chapter contains descriptions of qualities and techniques which caregivers may find helpful with other critically ill children. The techniques include creative and expressive opportunities such as guided-imagery activities used for stress and pain management, discussions, writing, and drawing. The personal qualities which were important to these children include trusting people to be truthful; feeling accepted in the moment, whether sick or playful, lighthearted or philosophical, practical or spiritual; and finally, living in an environment with hope (in an on-going although changing form) and of love, both received and expressed.

Personal qualities

Truth In Western culture there has been a tendency towards not telling children, and sometimes adults too, the truth about their illness. This comes about for a variety of reasons such as a wish to protect, a belief they do not know and would be further weakened if they were told, or that they do not wish to know the situation. Because these beliefs may be true for some individuals, it is critical to listen carefully to their questions in order to determine what their wishes are. It is equally critical that even when they do wish to know what the prognosis is, that they not be told in a blunt, or insensitive manner. Perhaps even more important is that information must always include hope; there should not be rigid certainty of outcome nor absolutes in time lines.

Finding the right way to handle such difficult situations is no easy task. In fact, caregivers need an effective support group for themselves because such a group provides an experienced audience both for exploring options of how to share such difficult topics with a child and for addressing the personal pain caregivers feel when they cannot prevent the inevitable. Witnessing the final phase of a child's journey in life can activate some strong issues for caregivers. To be most supportive one must be aware of personal material, so as not to project it into the relationship with the child. One must also have an outlet for the inevitable strain which at times arises from knowing the child's physical and psychological state.

Should a child ask, 'What will it be like when I die?' there is a clear indication the child already knows the outcome of the disease and is asking for honest communication. Because the intent underlying the questions can vary, a clarifying statement such as, 'You're wondering about the part of you that continues after the body dies,' or 'You're asking me what it's like to die,' helps direct further comments. Often what the child is really asking is, 'Can I talk to you about what's happening to me?' It could be that the child simply wants someone to talk with about feelings, especially fears, as well as about beliefs and physical condition. If this question is posed to family members, they may want to talk about personal beliefs of an afterlife, provided it is in a supportive manner. Presumably no one would frighten a child at this point with punitive beliefs inherent in some faiths. However, children often believe their disease is a punishment for a deed perceived as wrongful, and they need reassurance that God did not cause their illness because of some childhood act or thought.

If the question is posed to professionals, they can suggest that the child may want to talk with a parent about family beliefs, or they can explain the thoughts shared by other children; for example, they could say, 'Some children have told me they think there is no more pain after you die, and some have told me about going to a bright light where they will be very loved. Other kids have talked about going to meet someone they loved who died a long time before them.' Encouraging the children to describe what they believe is helpful. Such a discussion also allows dream experiences to be explored and provides an opening for talking about those things which are frightening or distressing.

Not only is the dying of a child terribly difficult for the adults helpless to prevent it, even the discussing of it can be devastating. With those caught in the taboo of never having explored personal issues about death, or with those too close to bear such a discussion, children usually know their difficulty and do not pose such questions. However, if a child has questions or thoughts which need openness, there should be someone available, and adults may need to specify who the child can talk to; for example, a parent could say, 'Lots of kids who have this disease have questions about it and about what's happening to them. Sometimes they just want to talk. If you ever want to talk to someone here in the hospital, Doctor Smith will be honest with you.' This permits the child to ask questions of someone knowledgeable, who has agreed to be open, and who will have an opportunity to maintain an on-going relationship of trust with the child. Young people indicate that having an adult to answer questions makes them feel 'like we're partners'. Having skilled listeners available provides young people the certainty that there's someone 'to confide in' and 'if there's something on my mind I can get it off my chest' (Krementz 1989).

Should a child ask a slightly different form of question such as, 'Am I going to die?' it may indicate a need to explore the possibility of death, or be a test of whether or not the adult will be truthful, or even be a way to confirm the reality of what the child already knows. The response needs to honest and age-appropriate, but never as a blunt 'Yes'. If the prognosis indicates the child will in all likelihood die from the disease, then putting that information in the context of all life forms may feel comfortable to the adult; for example,

> All the flowers die, all trees die, all the animals and birds die some time. All people die too. Great-grandma and Grandpa died a long time ago. Usually things die when they're very old, but sometimes they can get very, very sick and die when they're not so old. The doctors tell us what you have is very serious. They are trying all the medical things they can so you won't die, but right now they think that yes, you might die from this. We love you so very much and we will be with you all the time though. We'll keep trying the medicines and ideas

the doctors suggest and lots of times kids do get better from this.

It is important to note, however, that parents must have the final determination of what a child is told. One group of parents whose children had died from various diseases were asked what they would tell others going through a similar situation (Buckingham 1989). They encouraged parents to be honest with themselves and with their child.

Again, this is a very sensitive issue, and yet young people do want to know some things. If they have learned to protect parents, they may bring these questions to the medical community involved with their care. Bluebond-Langner describes a time when a child asked to borrow her tape recorder. Later that day, during a clinic meeting of those caring for the child, it came as quite a surprise to hear the warning tone her machine emitted as the tape ran out. The youngster wanted to know the truth about what was happening, and had resorted to surreptitiously taping adult meetings!

If parents are unable to talk about the probability of death with a child themselves, they may want to designate someone on the staff whom they trust to share appropriate, truthful information with the child. They may also tell the child to ask for more information from the staff or from a specific staff person. For example, they could say, 'You may have more questions than we can answer, so you might want to ask Dr Black or your Nurse, June, about some things.' Such an opening then gives the child permission to bring concerns into the open and facilitates communication. Prior to telling a child with whom to speak, the parents would, of course, have confirmed the individual's comfort with the topic.

There are several autobiographical books available written by children who have had life threatening illnesses, and they can be very helpful. Adults can read these for a greater understanding of the experience from the young person's perspective and can also read them with the child to explore commonalities. The material in *There is a Rainbow Behind Every Dark Cloud* addresses both the experience of serious illness and strategies for coping day-to-day. It includes text and drawings by the children themselves. *What It Feels Like to Fight for Your Life* is a series of fourteen autobiographical sketches with children and teens who have had life-threatening illness.

There are also children's classics such as *The Secret Garden* (Burnett 1911) and *Charlotte's Web* (White 1952) which address death and are very popular among critically ill children. Newer books such as *Remember the Secret* (Kübler-Ross 1982) and *Tom's Remembrance* (O'Hanlon Nunn 1987) give warm, loving images of existence beyond the physical form. Books such as these can be read together with the child or at least made available to them with a statement such as, 'Many kids who are sick like you find this book helps them. I'll leave it here and if you'd like to read it together or talk about it just let me know.' Such an opening allows honesty at whatever level the child prefers, and this may be exclusively in the third person as characters from the book are discussed. There will also be some children who are not yet ready to explore their illness at all, but they know someone who will be truthful is available if they change their minds.

As an indication of how much Rachel valued the truth, two of her creative works are shared here. First is a poem she had written early in her home teaching, while she was in remission. She had been taught the form for these cinquains and had written about her pets and the weather in previous ones. When asked to create one about a person, she wrote the following poem:

Gail
Happy, bubbly
Comforts sick kids
Tells the truth, trustful
Nurse

A spontaneous picture (Drawing 29) entitled 'The Scout's Honour' was drawn towards the end of Rachel's first school year at home, just as she was becoming consciously aware that she would die. The only comment Rachel cared to add to the picture was that the scout's motto was 'To tell the truth'. The house in this drawing appears to float above the large blue pickets; it has sky-blue lines in the middle; and it has a colourful column of smoke joining it to one ray of the sun. Given the precariousness of the house as it mingles with blue sky images, combined with the uncontained size of her tree as it spreads off the page, one can see the importance of telling the truth. There is little room for pretence or falsehood when one knows one's time on earth is limited.

Acceptance Children who experience life-threatening illness have a genuine need to express their pain and anger at times. Using swear words, for children who do not normally say these things, can have the powerful effect of releasing the tensions building in them. Their illness and all its resulting effects is an obscenity. By externalizing some of the rage and pain when these become overwhelming, rather than repressing them, children know they can continue to endure. Because such expressions are often offensive to other people, certain parameters can be set; for example, swearing takes place only when loud music is playing or in a certain room, and perhaps certain phrases are not permitted. Such limitations provide a form of containment for the intensity of the emotions. Other forms of expression can be used also: words can be written rather than said, old telephone books can be shredded or beaten, large cushions can be kicked or pounded, or foam bats can be used to hit a mattress. The important message for the children is that behaviour normally not permitted is allowed under the present circumstances, but still within certain limits.

Children must be allowed their sadness and fear also. The children themselves say things such as, 'Hiding your feelings just makes you more scared. It's okay to cry. It's okay to feel sorry for yourself and to be mad at the world and everyone in it' (Jampolsky & Taylor 1978, p. 51). Permitting expressions of these feelings provides children with the opportunity to release the emotions with an adult, and sometimes with other children, who are not afraid to witness their intensity. This experience makes the feelings more manageable because they then know they can cope with the feeling and not be consumed by it. Once they have learned to release feelings and not block them until they are truly overwhelming, young people can move to a more positive mindset, one of having some control, of fighting the disease and of enjoying each day as fully as possible.

By the same token, children need opportunities for joy and laughter also. Many hospitals have a humour channel or a children's channel with humourous programming for this purpose. Adolescents often use their own version of 'black humour' as a coping technique among themselves. Favourite storybooks, playful activities, the retelling of funny family stories all help to balance the difficult times at home and in hospital. The natural spontaneity of young people will provide these opportunities as long as the atmosphere permits.

Those closest to the child will know the moods well. While some children will seem very calm or stoic through much of the illness, adults need to allow the grumpy, non-cooperative times too. For some children, this aspect of their personality may need clear verbal permission or even encouragement. These feelings are often less accepted than more cheerful ones but they can be acknowledged in several ways. The adult can initiate the topic by saying something such as, 'You know, we all have bad days. It's okay to be cross and grumpy sometimes. You may want to talk with your teddy bear or throw crumpled paper balls. Even when you have a horrid day, we still love you.' Adults can provide books specific to feelings such as *Alexander and the Terrible, Horrible, No Good, Very Bad Day* (Viorst 1975) as a springboard for discussion. If it is comfortable for the adult, the child can be helped to explore a fantasy about being upset. In a totally accepting tone, the adult can reflect and even enthusiastically extend the image. Sometimes outrageous exaggeration within the dialogue helps the child vent tension just by building the image to the point of laughter at the ridiculous scene created together. When necessary, the adult may also remind the child about what is and what is not permitted in the outer world. Adults should describe specific outlets which are allowed, and they can use examples from children's books, movies and television as well as from their own lives to describe emotions strongly felt and appropriately expressed.

Love One of the more talked about feelings in much of the recent literature for health and medicine is love, specifically self-love. For children, feeling loved is always essential, but when they are vulnerable and fighting a life-threatening illness, love is critical. Feeling loved and accepted seems to nurture their spirit as well as their body, helping them cope with the struggle.

While any sudden increase in or unusual expressions of caring such as an abundance of new toys generates confusion, children do enjoy frequent reminders of their value. This can be as simple as a hug or statement that they are loved. It can be expressed in a note tucked into a sock to be found in the morning or in a bedtime ritual of saying a poem together.

Caregivers can be sure they make eye contact, use the child's name, and listen when asking how a child is. Taking a few minutes to share a common interest, such as bringing in a new stamp or tape or stuffed animal, or asking specifically about the outcome of a game or movie plot are minor in themselves, yet reflect caring about the child as an individual. Children frequently indicate that it is little touches such as these which make the difference in their sense of being cared for and being treated as real.

Children need to be allowed to give love also, which will mean others are asked to receive this love. The children who wrote in *There is a Rainbow Behind Every Dark Cloud* said, 'When you give help and love to others, it makes you feel warm and peaceful inside.' Like these children, Rachel too, frequently shared her loving nature. She often gave drawings to individuals important to her. Two common ways for her to express her feelings were to print 'Love ya' or to draw hearts in her pictures. One treasured example (Drawing 30) drawn seven weeks before she died, she titled 'Heart to Heart'. Seven, a number of totality (the three of the heavens and four of the earth, representing the spiritual and the temporal), is reflected in the hearts she drew. The intense red heart at the core is surrounded, halo-like, by a second solid yellow heart. It would appear to reflect her strong sense of both human and spiritual love.

Hope Kübler-Ross (1985) states that in giving a prognosis, one must always leave one per cent of hope. She indicates that hope may range from hope for a cure to hope of being accepted by God, but that maintaining hope is essential. Hope acts as one of the key threads in the evolving tapestry of the child's life; it provides the stability for life's fabric to continue as new 'fibres' or experiences are introduced.

Children who are facing life-threatening illnesses also express a similar belief in the need for hope. 'You always have to have a little hope because if you run out of that there's nothing worth anything. You might as well give up right then and there.' They indicate a belief that by modelling a positive attitude they may be able to help others cope, 'Hey, you know, maybe he's right, maybe there *is* hope'. They also come to recognize their own inner strength, 'One thing I can say for sure is that now I know how to fight for my life and never give up hope' (Krementz 1989).

For many of these children faith, often expressed in prayer, was part of this hope, 'Most of us found that praying was of great help. It made us not feel alone. It helped us to find faith and hope that we were safe.' Sometimes the hope was expressed more symbolically as the rainbow, 'And don't forget, when you have total Faith, that we are always connected to each other in love, you will surely find a rainbow on the other side of any dark cloud' (Jampolsky & Taylor 1978).

Expressive techniques

Expressive techniques allow unconscious content an opportunity to have form in the outer world. Dream images occur spontaneously once consciousness, or the ego, relinquishes control when the individual is sleeping. This, however, is a passive activity. In *Word and Image* Jung is quoted as saying, 'Images should be drawn or painted assiduously no matter whether you can do it or not' (Jaffé 1979, p. 116). The material thus produced is an active process, strengthening the bridge between the conscious and unconscious.

Most creative expressions from the unconscious have some form of approval from the ego to proceed even if it is only the volition to pick up a pencil and put a mark on the page, or even the permission to talk about certain material. The actual content released beyond this initial point is also influenced in varying degrees by conscious will. Because of this self-censorship, drawing seems to permit greater freedom of expression, especially for children who may not feel as comfortable with their written or verbal skills. The child's clarification or descriptions which are given following completion of the drawing are often freer than verbal material alone would have been because of the release which comes from the creative process itself. Words can then complement the visual image once it exists in the outer world.

As with any relationship, it is important for both the adult and the child to feel comfortable with the expressive activity being used. For some individuals enactment through play will seem most effective. For others, creating a changing world in the sand tray will be the best outlet. Some people prefer body movement or music and others enjoy the sensory experience of modelling clay or playdough. Oaklander (1978) provides a huge selection of specific activities to use with children, but often just providing the materials for them to use encourages their self-expression.

As seriously ill children become less mobile and less energetic, they may prefer other expressive activities. Instead of creative play using the full range of toys, they may benefit from using puppets or from just telling a story about them. These children often derive great pleasure from telling the story or giving captions to a book using photographs. They can use existing family photos, and they truly enjoy taking photographs themselves for such a book.

Other books can be collections of their work from a variety of sources simply compiled in scrapbook form. There is a clear visual representation of who they are when various graphics are bound together. Audio and videotape recordings of their experiences and thoughts are other forms some children like to direct in relation to themselves. The underlying consideration for all of these is to provide an opportunity for the unconscious to be expressed in the outer world in some valued way.

Because it is evident that children do have an inner awareness of their prognosis, but may not understand it in the context of their concrete, confusing and painful experiences, the adults who care for them can help by making some expressive opportunities available to them. Thus, consciousness can also develop some insight and comfort.

Discussions As indicated previously, an opportunity to ask questions is very important for many children facing life-threatening illnesses. The responses to these questions can make an incredible difference in whether the child feels alone and fearful or supported and understood. At times children will ask these questions of adults and at other times of their peers. When an adult is responding, it is important to be honest, to use age-appropriate language, and to respond to what has really been asked. Clarification of what the question is about allows the adults to be certain they are not projecting their own assumptions or concerns into the conversation. Letting the child be the guide to the duration and content of the discussion also indicates respect for the child's needs.

More structured group discussions also help young people with a variety of issues which arise as a result of facing life-threatening illnesses. The sharing of common disease-related experiences and of coping strategies is of great value. 'We found it helpful to find other kids who have similar problems and to meet with them. We have found that, as we helped each other, we have helped ourselves . . . It is helpful to find you are not alone, and that there are other kids just like you who are going through the same thing . . . Kids can be more helpful than adults because they talk your language. Kids can also understand without your having to use words' (Jampolsky & Taylor 1978, p. 51).

Although the material in their book arose from group work at the Centre for Attitudinal Healing, Jampolsky and Taylor have compiled the actual drawings and comments from participants in a way that allows other children to use it almost as if they too are group members. Young people can read what the participants said, see some of their drawings, and then add their own drawings to the book on the pages and topics provided. It is an excellent resource.

Writing Some children enjoy the use of words for self-expression and may find a great deal of release through written activities. This may include keeping a journal, writing letters or poetry, completing sentence stems or dictating stories. They may prefer to tell a story about pictures provided for them, about photographs of themselves and family or about their own art work. Many children seem to feel most comfortable telling about their own creations. However, if there is no response to a request such as, 'Can you tell me about the drawing?' one must respect the importance of the picture for the valuable image that it is.

Sentence stems are brief, flexible and often reveal how the child views the world or what they hope to find in others. For example, Rachel chose to complete several stems for 'A Friend Is . . .'

A friend is helpful
A friend is kind
A friend is loving
A friend is gentle
A friend is willing
A friend is welcoming

which reflect her own qualities.

Several authors (Allan & Bertoia 1992, Buckingham 1989, Krementz 1989, Kübler-Ross 1983) share activities and examples of children's written material created during difficult times. Encouraging children to write or to dictate their creative works provides them with an outlet for some of the pain and turmoil they experience as well as for some of the wisdom and perceptiveness they develop.

Imagery and relaxation Another valuable technique is guided imagery which can be used for relaxation and pain management. Kiddie QR© (Stroebel, Stroebel & Holland 1980) is an easy to use programme based on the Relaxation Response developed by Benson. Using a variety of relaxation and guided-imagery activities which can be read or listened to on tape, the child learns a series of physiological responses within the body. Several suggested activities are useful for extending the expressive images, and drawings are especially valuable to help caregivers understand the child. One of these has the children trace one foot and draw the 'Magic Breathing Holes' previously visualized during the lesson's relaxation activity. In Rachel's example (Drawing 31) she again demonstrated her unconscious insights by drawing an eye on the sole of her traced foot; the eye is seen symbolically as a mirror of the soul (Herder 1986). Just beneath the eye is a large orange 'breathing hole' with many smaller blue ones scattered over the sole.

Another activity, 'The Bubble Pipe', directs the children to imagine each of their distressing experiences and emotions being released within a separate bubble as they exhale. Sometimes they even visualize the filled bubbles floating off into the sky. As a follow-up they can create a drawing of the pipe and bubbles. Children can also use this visual image in combination with a focus on their breathing during medical procedures. In some hospitals actual soap bubbles are created by a parent or clinician to reinforce the image and to help distract the child undergoing difficult procedures.

A rather dramatic example of guided imagery combined with a drawing shows the relationship (Drawing 32) between psyche and soma. Rachel was first taken through a specific relaxation and guided-imagery activity of what it was like to be a rosebush and then asked to draw herself as one (Oaklander 1978, Allan 1988). Following the drawing, Rachel was asked if she could describe her picture. The unusual feature was the somewhat unique appearance of three bushes, rather than a single one. Rachel indicated that the bush on the right with lollipops but no leaves was from 'Candyland', a special place from a previous guided imagery. The central bush was crying because the crows were eating all the buds before they could blossom. The rosebush on the left, drawn with the long blonde hair Rachel often drew on figures associated with herself, was happy because it was blooming. However, if one looks at the trajectory of the crows near the top of the page, they are both aimed at the happy bush. This reflected the state of Rachel's blood work two days later, which indicated she was no longer in remission. Again, although there was no verbal indication she knew of her health status, the content of the drawing suggests the unconscious did know what was happening in her body. This activity is enjoyed by children and provides much information to the caregiver.

Another way of using imagery is in active imagination. Some children indicate, 'We found that, by using our imagination, we could keep a picture in our mind of a rainbow on the other side of a stormy cloud. This helped give us hope and patience' (Jampolsky & Taylor 1978, p. 63). These children and many others found the Simonton techniques of visualization for combating the disease cells and for healing to be very helpful. Many young people also find visualizations or guided imagery useful to 'see' themselves doing something or being somewhere they enjoy, for releasing distressing emotions, and for experiencing positive, loving scenarios. There is great value in having the mind create a desired situation within the individual.

Drawings As indicated previously, drawings can be done on a directed basis, where the adult suggests the child create a specific drawing, or they can be completely spontaneous where the child chooses to draw without any prompting. The latter can be in the presence of the adult or even while the child is alone. Although the discussion here is related to drawn or coloured images, some children prefer to do collage work or use materials such as modelling clay.

One example of an impromptu drawing (Drawing 33) was created on a day Rachel was feeling especially ill. Although she had had a bad night and still felt ill in the morning, the teacher had not been notified prior to arrival at Rachel's home, and so planned just to speak to Rachel briefly and then leave. However, after a little reflective listening, the teacher asked Rachel if she would like to draw. Rachel replied in the affirmative and decided to draw a picture of how she was feeling. As she worked on the drawing she also spoke, 'Boy wait till you see how sick I feel . . . wait till you see how upset my stomach is!'

In this drawing Rachel duplicated the upset facial expressions as a second one in her stomach, with the addition of the small amount of chicken noodle soup she had been able to eat for breakfast. One of the most interesting features of this picture is related to the title. When asked if it had a title, Rachel replied, 'Yes, not feeling well.' Yet when asked who would record the title, Rachel wrote it herself as 'not feeling bad'. When the teacher noted the difference between the dictated and written titles, Rachel replied, 'I got it all out in the picture.' Such 'slips' indicate just how knowledgeable the unconscious is of the status of the body. Once the discrepancy was pointed out to Rachel, her conscious self also recognized the new physical condition as indicated by her next words, she asked if the teacher could stay and if they could do the most challenging academic subjects. In this example, it seems as if the drawing process provided release of some of the upset feelings, at least the emotional ones and it would appear some physical distress was released also. In addition, the verbal/written component indicates the strong relationship between the unconscious and somatic aspects of the child. Drawings can be useful not only for what they indicate, but also as a mechanism for release.

Some of the impromptu drawings Rachel made were used intentionally as an opportunity to vent feelings. The teacher would routinely ask, 'Would you like to do a drawing?' and on one occasion, when assured she could do whatever she wanted Rachel asked, 'Even lines and scribbles?' This exchange allowed Rachel to do exactly that, at times creating strong colours with some pressure and other times making images which flowed more evenly. One example is 'The Chinese Boat on the High Seas' (Drawing 34) created when Rachel appeared to be feeling somewhat contemplative but was not concentrating on school. She began with blue horizontal lines and then moved to yellow jagged ones vertically crossing the page. Several other colours were used, some smudged on top of each other, with increasing energy as she worked. She finished with red lines and then dark orange loops across the page. After completing the picture she was asked if it had a title. She turned it around a full 360 degrees, announced the title was 'The Chinese Boat on the High Seas' and then asked for the name of the small boats seen in photographs of the Orient. When asked if it could be 'junks' she indicated that was the right word. A small portion of the bottom centre suggested a junk to her. She described a news story she and her family had seen on television of a similar boat being tossed about in a storm as refugees fled their country. At a symbolic level, this could certainly reflect the stormy time created by her disease as well as the theme of her own tempestuous journey, ultimately leading her to a new land.

Two other examples of spontaneous drawings were created while Rachel was in hospital for the final time. She simply drew these on her own and then gave them to her family. One picture (Drawing 35) is of two hills, each with a building on it. A black car on the left hill is angled towards the valley, as if heading into the sunset. (A nurse who was present asked if the sun was rising or setting.) The two smokeless houses suggest Rachel's leaving – either her two childhood homes, or perhaps her current home and the hospital also. Jung compares a life cycle to the path of the sun. It rises at birth from the horizon and moves one hundred and eighty degrees in an arc to set again at the horizon at the time of death. This picture clearly indicates Rachel's imminent departure.

The other drawing (Drawing 36) shows all but one deciduous tree in full foliage in January and a robin that has left the nest. This robin on the ground is looking off to the left of the page. The little worm looking from the bottom left towards the robin appears disconcerted. Yet, although in ordinary circumstances a robin would actively seek the worm as food, here something more compelling has momentarily drawn the robin's attention. The worm, an inhabitant of the ground and symbolically seen both as death/dissolution and awakening from death, is clearly visible above ground; the robin, symbolic of death and resurrection, may still consume the worm. By ingesting the worm, the robin would be able to integrate their death images; although physical dissolution may occur, there is a clear awareness of the reawakening of spiritual form.

It is interesting to note that Rachel drew a baby robin in the nest hatching from its egg in November, and she drew a mature robin leaving the nest two months later in January. These events are not in their normal seasons. It seems as if her resurrected spirit is born and matures even as her body faces its winter season, death. The life of the robin does not follow nature's expected cycle any more than Rachel's death while still a child matches the natural order of humanity. Even her purely recreational drawings show that Rachel clearly knew, consciously as well as unconsciously, what her destiny was; and she used expressive opportunities to help integrate the two.

The drawn and written works created by so many children such as Rachel help caregivers grasp the depth of wisdom and insight these children experience by facing life-threatening illnesses. When the final outcome is a transition to a form of existence we know so little about, the young people seem to 'know' that also. Their works help caregivers define ways in which to be most helpful and valuable to them while they are completing this portion of their journeys. By responding to what the children indicate is needed and desired, caregivers can honour their struggle. By providing more than the traditional physical support given so generously, by giving expressive opportunities as well as love, hope, truth and acceptance, caregivers can ease the burden these young people carry. This additional support ultimately seems to help the young people find some form of meaning in their experience, often as the development of their own spirituality. These children become teachers of life and they leave a powerful gift.

Glossary

Because a few terms are used frequently throughout the book they are defined here to provide ready access for the reader without being cumbersome within the text.

Decathexis This refers to a diminishing investment of energy being directed into attachments. Throughout life the child has put considerable emotional energy into relationships and attachments to people, pets, favourite toys, places, and so forth. With death approaching, everything must be left behind and the child must gradually detach from them. Decathexis will have two aspects. One will be the awareness of death reflected in various death images, and the other will be separation or distancing from all attachments.

The dying must separate from everyone and everything they love, from this world and even from their own bodies. There is a decreasing interest in wordly events, a sense that these things do not matter as much anymore. There are often images in dreams or drawings of physical separation and distancing such as travel or barriers. There is also a need to recognize and deal with the deterioration of the body which will lead to death and force the separations. As the disease progresses and the body fails and experiences pain, the children gradually move towards an awareness of the dissolution of the 'shell' they have inhabited and to which they are so attached. The task of decathexis then is a difficult one of separating from all things of this world.

Directed or impromptu drawings These are drawings created following a request from another person, either for a specific topic such as a for a house (directed drawing) or simply for a picture, 'Would you like to draw a picture?' (impromptu drawing).

Rebirth This refers to some form of transcending death, of being reborn into some new frame of existence or attitude about life. In this sense, the rebirth also applies to the development of tolerance for the dying process and for what happens after this body dies. For many people it will be a clearer spiritual awareness of whatever they believe happens following biological death. This belief may manifest as religious images, as a form of continuation in this world within the memories of others, or as a specific contribution such as a poem written for a loved one or tree planted with great care. It can also appear as some other personal belief system which provides comfort. The development of the rebirth awareness or of a new attitude towards dying allows for some degree of mental well-being; otherwise all the emotions surrounding the approaching death and total separation could be overwhelming. It also reflects the on-going nature and existence of the inner psyche or spiritual aspect of the individual. This transformation or rebirth can provide for a relatively peaceful transition into death, and at times the images are filled with joy.

Spontaneous drawings These are drawings initiated by an individual without any stimulus from another person.

Stages of illness The five stages which follow have been defined by Bluebond-Langner (1978) based on her study of hospitalized, terminally ill children:

Stage 1: Seriously ill The children have thought of themselves as well until symptoms necessitated hospital admission for tests. This experience and reactions of family to the diagnosis leads to a new view of self as being 'seriously ill'. This view of self persists until there is evidence they are getting better.

Stage 2: Seriously ill and will get better Regular out-patient clinic visits for treatment result in the children learning about various drugs and their effects, often from conversations with other children. In Stage 2, the drugs have made them feel better and most people treat them normally again.

Stage 3: Always ill and will get better Following the first relapse the children's view of self changes again, to always being ill. However, once the children are in remission again, the parents and the children come to believe that one can be sick many times, but one can still recover.

Stage 4: Always ill and will never get better More relapses, drug complications, and on-going pain force the children to see themselves as always ill and never being completely better.

Stage 5: Dying Once children who are in Stage 4 hear about the death of a peer from the same disease, they move into Stage 5. In various forms, either overt statements or through symbolic verbal and nonverbal images, the children indicate that they know they are dying.

Symbolic language This refers to both conscious and unconscious forms of communication which send the desired message, but which may or may not be clear to the recipient. For example, symbolic verbal language may be expressed in words but stated as a metaphor for the intended concept; the phrase 'the penny dropped' is a way of saying insight has been gained. Behaviour and other nonverbal language such as posture and facial expression may convey feeling; play may be an enactment of psychological material; and drawings often use concrete images to represent inner issues.

Appendix A
Story text and teacher notes

Text for Drawing 1

I'm walking in the forest and it's the last part of the forest and I see this bush walking up to me and I know it was Andrea tricking me. Then I saw Derek up in the tree. Then I thought, 'Andrea is playing a bad trick and any minute she'll jump up.'

So then I went over to the bush and looked in and I saw Andrea. She said, 'How did you know I was in here?'

I said, 'I didn't.' And then I saw Derek and he asked how I knew he was there and I said I didn't. Then they put spiders all over me and I screamed all the way home.

Text for Drawing 2

These little kids were playing hide-and-go-seek in the forest and all of them hid in a tree because a hungry wolf was coming by. And they were scared and ran away and it scared him too. And he never came back again.

There's a hole and those are the holes in the trees where the kids are hiding.

Text for Drawing 3

Well she's crying because she just fell on the gravel and she scratched all up on her knee. She's also crying because her mother told her not to go out. She's always crying. She's also crying because the guys don't like her and also she's crying because her Mom promised to take her to Disneyland and she didn't.

Comments

Rachel: I want to use pencil today.
Teacher: She's really sad.
Rachel: Yes.
Teacher: Can you tell me about her sad feelings?
Rachel: Dictated story above.

[Forty-five minutes earlier she talked about the night before: 'I had a really bad night last night. I couldn't walk. Mom had to carry me and my legs felt like they weren't there. I felt really dizzy. It was scary!']

Text for Drawing 4

Once upon a time there was a Rainbow Bright Google. And he was wandering by the castle in the tall grass. And it was a beautiful day out like it was all the time. And he realized he was outside, 'cause he was only one year old. And it was a beautiful castle he was standing by. And he thought to himself, 'Is this my home?' And he went in and he realized it was.

Text for Drawing 5

There was these people. They just retired and they felt like a little break. So they went out in the country where the wild life lived.

And at night they sort of got a little scared, but not that scared because deer and fawns came up to their windows and the animals started to love them. And so they decided to live there. And they lived happily ever after.

Text for Drawing 6

One day a girl named Melody went to the zoo. And she saw a gorilla. And these people were feeding him oranges, apples, carrots and bananas. And there was even a mirror and a swing there. And there were strong bars. He looked fierce.

Text for Drawing 7

There was an art gallery and this punky girl made a design on the picture. It looked like scribbles, but it wasn't. It was eyes. It looked like scribbles, but it was actually eyes. One day she came in to the gallery and one of the eyes winked at her. Then she thought, 'Somebody's tricking me.' Then the picture said, 'Nobody's tricking you.' She looked around. 'Who said that?' Then the picture said, 'I did.' Then she woke up.

Comments

Rachel: It's framed.
Teacher: This purple line is the frame.
Rachel: Yes.

Text for Drawing 8

Once upon a time there was this girl named Suzanne. It was night time. Suzanne was walking. She had run away and she saw this house. It was a patchy house. It had white, really bright blue, and black and brown patches on it. She thought, 'I think it's empty. No one lives in it. I think I'll live there for a while.' She went in and saw this creaky stairway. She went up, creak, creeak, creeeak, creaak. And a ghost looked around the corner and said, 'There's a trespasser in the house.' But this was just a trick. But she didn't know that. So she went to sleep. The ghost came and scared her and she woke up and screamed. She saw a hole in the roof. She jumped as high as she could and just caught the edge of the hole and pushed herself up. And there she saw her lost brother. He had ran away years before.

The End.

Comments

Rachel: These ghosts don't need eyes [pointed to three ghosts in windows]. Ghosts can see without eyes.

Text for Drawing 9

Once there was a man. He went down in a barrel. And he woke up from his dream and he got into a barrel and did the same thing as in his dreams. He broke a leg. He woke up in the hospital. He wondered what happened. And he lived on.

Comments

She drew the rocks first, and later went over them again doubling their size. As she drew, she said it was a waterfall. She spoke of travelling, of Niagara Falls and then Disneyland. She specified the Frog ride in Disneyland and how hot it was in the 'Hell' part of that ride. As she was talking, she coloured in all the blue part of the page.
[Earlier Rachel had been speaking about a news story of a man who had gone over Niagara Falls in a barrel.]

Text for Drawing 10

The Rabbit Disguise

Once there was a man and he loved carrots. And he was looking for work. And he spotted a store with a rabbit suit. So he bought the rabbit suit. And he loved carrots – you have to remember that! He lived in a cabin in the forest. There was only one carrot in that whole forest that every rabbit was trying to get to. Now this rabbit suit was very large, bigger than all the other rabbits. And when he got to that carrot all these other rabbits began coming. When they saw him they scadoodeled! And he ate the carrot.

Comments

Rachel: I want to draw a picture. I used to draw really good rabbits, but I don't now. I've changed. I want to use pen only.
[As she drew she talked about her best friend, who had just died on Saturday. 'She loved me best.']

Text for Drawing 11

The Flower Bed

Rachel: I want to do it in pencil.
There was much erasing of the flower on the right, as her friend's funeral was discussed. She said all the flowers were different, and identified the one on the right as a tulip when it was finished.

She volunteered that the birds were [as she pointed left to right] 'crows', 'robins', and 'eagles', then changed her mind and identified the middle ones as 'hawks', not 'robins' [crows, hawks, eagles].

Text for Drawing 12

The Sad Monster

Teacher: Does it have a title?
Rachel: The Sad Monster. He's sad because he wants buddies, he's saying, 'I want to be buddies.' These ones say, 'Yes' but this one says, 'No'.

Comments

Rachel spoke of her best friend's funeral which was being held that day and said, 'Who wants to see a coffin.'

As she was drawing, she spoke of her friendship with the teacher and wanted to discuss the reason why we have funerals.

Text for Drawing 13

A Chinese man is pulling a flower cart and he gets a flat tire. He says, 'Oh no, a flat tire.'

Text for Drawing 14

No story or title.

Text for Drawing 15

Time Machine

Teacher: Does it have a title?
Rachel: The Time Machine.
Teacher: Can you tell me about the time machine.
Rachel: You can go forward or backwards. [Pointed to the red spots] These two red buttons are the controls. I've had a good life. I don't want to see the future.

Text for Drawing 16

Beware of Ghost!

Teacher: Can you tell me about the picture.
Rachel: The bird is looking at the house, 'I want to get outa here.' [The tree without leaves] 'I'm cold.' It never had any leaves. [The ghost, lower right] 'I'm going to get that bird and eat him.' [The fence] 'I hurt.' 'Cause it's all broken.

The house has boards over the holes. It has broken windows. 'I'm scary.' The attic window's not broken. That's where the ghost lives. It's nice and clean there in that room.

[The tree leaning towards the house] It's a covering tree. The mud puddles are there because there's just been a big, bad storm with thunder and lightning.

[The moon] 'What a scary place! I don't even like to look at it!'

Text for Drawing 17

Monster

Teacher: Do you ever feel like that little person calling for help?
Rachel: Promise you won't tell Mom and Dad, I don't want to worry them.

We spoke at length about her concern for the family's difficult time with her being sick and about spiritual matters. She initiated a variety of topics.

Text for Drawing 18

The Baby Robin
Rachel said she had seen this robin outside her window that morning.

Text for Drawing 19

Apple Core
No story.

Text for Drawing 20

Land and Sea
The princess is being carried back to the king's castle [upper left] so she can TELL him she's going to marry the slave. Then they're going back to Castlegar to get married and go to Nelson to live.
Teacher: She can tell him she's going to marry the slave.
Rachel: She can tell him because she's twenty.

Text for Drawing 21

Bear in the Snow
Fred bear lives with his Mom and Dad in a warm, happy hut. He came out on a cloudy day to build a snowman.

Comments

Rachel spent much of her time erasing the bear. 'I can't get him light enough,' was her comment.

Text for Drawing 22

Rainbow of Light
No story.

Text for Drawing 23

Fat and Little
No story.

Text for Drawing 24

The Ice Capades
Teacher: Can you tell me about this picture?
Rachel: Well, that's me and my sister's boyfriend [upper centre]. He took me to the Ice Capades. They had on these costumes and they had to jump over this great big hole in the middle of the ice.

Text for Drawing 25

The Secret Garden
Me and my Mom are reading this book.

Teacher:	Can you tell me about the secret garden?
Rachel:	Well, right now you can see the door and the doorknob, but after a while the green stuff [asked for name of stuff that grows up walls – ivy] yeah, the ivy will cover the whole wall and then it will be really hard to find the door.

Text for Drawing 26

No story or title.

Text for Drawing 27

My Squiggle
No story.

Text for Drawing 28

Zig Zag
No story.

Appendix B
Expert classification

For those readers interested in the original research related to the first twenty-eight drawings and their content, the following material is presented here in appended form:

Appendix B	– a written summary of the experts' task and their findings.
Appendix C	– the direction and information sheet given to the experts.
Appendix D	– the Drawing Category Record Form
Appendix E	– a table showing the chronological order of the figures matched to the random order seen by experts.
Appendix F	– a table showing the actual categorizations by each expert for each drawing and the percentage frequency of each drawing for each category.

Description of experts' task

The second approach to drawing analysis was to have experts in the use of drawings read each picture with its accompanying text and choose one of three categories for each picture. Six experts, one from Switzerland, one from the United States, one from Alberta, and three from British Columbia, were interviewed and asked to look at each of the twenty-eight drawings. An expert was defined as someone who had a degree in the helping professions, had been trained specifically in the interpretation of drawings and had had a minimum of five years experience. The experts were asked to determine whether or not they would classify each drawing, based on its content, into one of three categories: Decathexis, Rebirth, or not applicable. The last category was included to allow for placement of those pictures which have no other obvious placement.

Each expert was seen individually and given the set of drawings and an information sheet (see Appendix C) with background information, definitions and directions for using the drawing classification sheet (see Appendix D).

The results of the classifications were summarized in the research document and per cent of agreement about each picture was calculated. This was followed by a discussion about their findings.

Summary of findings

The experts worked on the drawings in a randomized order, not the chronological sequences described previously (see Appendix E, Table 1, for corresponding random/chronological order). They had been given the information sheet (see Appendix C) for general background and had the text and teacher notes (see Appendix A) to accompany each drawing. These had been matched to the random order sequence received by the experts. Therefore, they worked with each picture in isolation, not knowing the date of any drawing nor which one came before or after another.

They approached the task in different ways, some sorting the drawings into related stacks, then naming the category afterwards, and some naming each picture's category as they viewed it. Some spread all the pictures out in front of them and sorted from easier to more difficult to classify. One sorted solely by pictures, then confirmed the classifications using the text – and found complete agreement with the original sort. Others used the text only to clarify ambiguous drawing content, and some used the text routinely as a supplement to the drawing content. The comments of the experts as they worked provided insights as to how they initially saw the image and what it activated in them before they read the text. One expert commented on the similarity of the 'Fat and Little' drawing and the untitled drawing of the two butterflies with floating trees as being very similar to those of other leukemic children with whom the expert had worked. As they articulated their thinking, it became evident that they were first attracted to different parts within the same drawing. For example, one expert who first noted the flower cart in Drawing 13 spoke of the design of the flowers, but another expert who also first noted the flower cart, saw its flat tire and commented on the resemblance of the tire to a camera. One expert saw the gorilla in Drawing 6 as a bear, another read the title of 'My squiggle' as 'My struggle' reflecting the tension in the drawing. One saw the time machine as a rainbow cave and another saw it as a tunnel. Two saw the abstract Drawing 26 as looking like a mandala. Two experts commented on the frequency of unusual eyes in the drawings and two on the frequency of plants and animals. Most mentioned one or two images which impacted especially on them and all commented on the touching beauty of 'The Baby Robin' drawing.

Of the twenty-eight drawings sorted by the experts (see Appendix F, Table 2) there was agreement of 83 per cent or higher on eighteen of them. Seven drawings were unanimously placed: the crying girl, the art gallery and 'The Sad Monster' as Decathexis drawings, and the recreational vehicle, the butterflies, 'The Baby Robin' and 'Rainbow of Light' as Rebirth. Two-thirds of the experts agreed on the placements for twenty-four of the twenty-eight drawings. Generally, those drawings for which there was most disagreement were spread throughout the series, but there were four in a row, numbers 23 ('The Ice Capades') to 26 ('My Squiggle'), near the end of the series which had little agreement in placement. The experts' sorting matched the researcher's in tending to place more of Rachel's drawings after the mid-point in the series, after she became consciously aware she would die from the disease, in the category of rebirth.

The experts all commented in some form about how challenging the task was. They noted especially that some pictures contained images of both Decathexis and Rebirth and, therefore, they had to determine which had ascendency. The following sixteen numbers were voluntarily identified by only one person each as containing dual images: 1, 3, 4, 8, 9, 10, 12, 13, 14, 17, 18, 19, 20, 21, 24, and 28. It is interesting to note how few were seen by more than one person as containing images from both categories: two experts saw numbers 9 and 28 as having dual images and three saw 10 and 20 that way. Having a category defined as 'Both' would have avoided the difficulty, but a forced choice format helps clarify the dominant images from the drawings.

One expert had anticipated that many of the drawings would

contain images which were not applicable to the two main categories, and which would instead reflect more of the events currently happening in the child's everyday world. This expert and one other who did use the 'not applicable' category indicated that the drawings sorted into this category did not have clear placement in either of the other two. They considered each of these drawings carefully before choosing the category. One expert who considered Rachel's last drawing for quite a while before choosing 'not applicable' commented that 'She has obviously resolved something here'.

It would seem that it is possible to obtain a fairly good level of agreement among those who are trained to read drawings when they are asked to sort into specific categories. The process of arriving at the decision varies considerably however. It was clear that the experts also noted the difficulty of determining the death/rebirth delineation. Also clear was that no matter what the intended topic for the drawing was, the unconscious issues related to a changing view of self as dying and as being reborn into a new view of self were evident to those trained in reading drawings.

Appendix C
Information sheet

This research is investigating the experience of a terminally ill child. Part of the research will be based on how adults classify the drawings from one such child. It is hoped that the research will assist with an understanding of a dying child's experience.

Your task

There are twenty-eight drawings in random order. You are asked to look at each of the drawings provided along with its accompanying printed material, and decide which of three categories defined below seems to you to be the most appropriate placement for it. Thus, for picture '1' you could judge the category 'decathexis', 'not applicable' or 'rebirth', as the most likely placement.

Please place the picture's number under the category title you believe is the best choice for it.

Definitions

The following explanations are based on the assumption that, at some point, terminally ill children are aware that they are dying.

Decathexis

This refers to a diminishing investment of energy being directed into attachments. In the past the child has put considerable emotional energy into relationships and attachments to people, pets, favourite toys, places, etc. With death approaching, everything must be left behind and the child must gradually detach from them. Decathexis then will have two aspects. One will be the awareness of death reflected in various death images, and the other will be separation or distancing from all attachments.

The dying must separate from everyone and everything they love, from this world and even from their own bodies. There is a decreasing interest in wordly events, a sense that these things do not matter as much anymore. There are images of physical separation and distancing such as travel or barriers. There is also a need to recognize and deal with the deterioration of the body which will lead to death and force the separations. As the disease continues and the body fails and is in pain, the children gradually move towards an awareness of the dissolution of the 'shell' they've inhabited and are so attached to. The task of decathexis then is a difficult one of separating from all things of this world.

Not applicable

If both 'decathexis' and 'rebirth' seem inappropriate for any picture, the middle category 'not applicable' is available.

Rebirth

This refers to some form of transcending death, of being reborn into some new frame of existence. In this sense, the rebirth also applies to the development of some form of tolerance for the dying process and for what happens after this body dies. For many it will be a clearer spiritual awareness of whatever they believe happens following biological death. This may manifest as religious images, as a form of continuation in this world within the memories of others, or as a specific contribution such as a poem written for a loved one or tree planted with great care. It can also appear as some other personal belief system which provides comfort. The development of the rebirth awareness allows for some degree of mental well being; otherwise all the emotions surrounding the approaching death and total separation could be overwhelming. This transformation or rebirth can provide for a relatively peaceful transition into death, and at times the images are filled with joy.

History

The child who did these drawings had been diagnosed as having leukaemia when she was six years old. She completed grades one and two at school. Her home schooling began in September when she was seven, in grade three. The researcher was then a home/hospital teacher who worked with the child for a year and half. These drawings were done as part of her regular schooling, usually within language arts. The drawings included here were done when she was eight and nine. She died of leukaemia in January, a month and a half after her ninth birthday.

In each of the drawing sessions represented here, the child was given no specific direction, only asked if she would like to 'draw a picture'. She had a consistent choice of materials and content each time, although the quality of paper available varied from session to session. There was a choice of pen, pencil, felt pens, pencil crayons and pastels.

Following each drawing she was asked if the picture had a title and a story. These were recorded, as was the date. When there was no information given, specific comments were made to elicit some detail, such as, 'Can you tell me about this part?' The verbal information has been typed and is attached to the drawing. Her comments noted during the drawing are also included. Although she completed sixty drawings from February to the following January, only twenty-eight are included here, partly because of concern for the amount of time you would need to classify all of them and partly because the content of many was influenced by family or other adults.

Conclusion

This researcher is aware that your challenge is a formidable one. You may use your experience, intuition and training for it. This particular categorizing of pictures has not been done before so your work is unique, and it is most appreciated. Thank you!

Appendix D
Drawing category record form

DECATHEXIS	NOT APPLICABLE	REBIRTH

Appendix E
Table 1

Chronological order matched to random order seen by experts

Drawing number		*Random number*	*Drawing number*		*Random number*
1	–	13	15	–	9
2	–	20	16	–	25
3	–	2	17	–	6
4	–	10	18	–	16
5	–	8	19	–	26
6	–	7	20	–	5
7	–	20	21	–	4
8	–	15	22	–	12
9	–	3	23	–	21
10	–	1	24	–	23
11	–	22	25	–	24
12	–	14	26	–	19
13	–	27	27	–	11
14	–	17	28	–	18

Appendix F
Table 2

Expert classification of random drawings according to decathexis (D), not applicable (NA) and rebirth (R)

Drawing	*Expert*						*Summary*		
	1	2	3	4	5	6	% D	% NA	% R
1	D	D	R	D	D	D	83	–	17
2	D	D	D	D	D	D	100	–	–
3	D	D	R	D	R	D	67	–	33
4	D	D	D	D	D	R	83	–	17
5	R	D	R	R	R	R	17	–	83
6	R	D	D	D	D	R	67	–	33
7	R	D	NA	D	D	D	67	17	17
8	R	R	R	R	R	R	–	–	100
9	D	D	D	R	D	D	83	–	17
10	R	R	R	D	R	R	17	–	83
11	D	D	D	D	D	R	83	–	17
12	R	R	R	R	R	R	–	–	100
13	D	D	NA	D	D	D	83	17	–
14	D	D	D	D	D	D	100	–	–
15	R	D	D	D	R	R	50	–	50
16	R	R	R	R	R	R	–	–	100
17	R	R	R	R	R	R	–	–	100
18	R	R	NA	R	R	R	–	17	83
19	D	R	D	R	R	R	33	–	67
20	D	D	D	D	D	D	100	–	–

Table 2 *continued*

Drawing	*Expert*						*Summary*		
	1	2	3	4	5	6	% D	% NA	% R
21	D	NA	NA	R	D	R	33	33	33
22	R	R	D	R	R	D	33	–	67
23	R	NA	D	R	D	R	33	17	50
24	D	R	D	D	R	R	50	–	50
25	D	D	D	D	R	D	83	–	17
26	D	D	D	R	D	R	67	–	33
27	D	D	D	R	D	D	83	–	17
28	R	D	D	D	D	D	83	–	17

Table 2 shows each expert's classification of every drawing. The three summary columns on the right side show the percentage of experts who placed the drawing in each category.

References

Allan, J. (1978) 'Serial drawing: A therapeutic approach with young children', *Canadian Counsellor* 12, 223–228.

—— (1988) *Inscapes of the Child's World: Jungian Counseling in the Schools*, Dallas, TX: Spring Publications, Inc.

Allan, J. & Bertoia, J. (1992) *Written Paths to Healing: Education and Jungian Child Counseling*, Dallas, TX: Spring Publications, Inc.

Bach, S. (1966) 'Spontaneous paintings of severely ill patients', *Acta Psychosomatica*, 8: 1–66.

—— (1975) 'Spontaneous pictures of leukemic children as an expression of the total personality, mind, and body', *Acta Paedopsychiatrica*, 41: 86–104.

—— (1977, March) Guidelines for reading and evaluating spontaneous pictures, *International Study Group*, Zurich, Switzerland.

—— (1990) *Life Paints Its Own Span*, Einsiedeln, Switzerland: Daimon Verlag.

Bertoia, J. (1990) Drawings from a dying child: A case study approach, unpublished MA thesis, University of British Columbia, Vancouver, BC.

Bertoia, J. & Allan, J. (1988) 'Counseling seriously ill children: Use of spontaneous drawings', *Elementary School Guidance and Counseling*, 22: 206–221.

Betz, C.L. & Poster, E.C. (1984) 'Children's concepts of death: Implications for pediatric practice', *Nursing Clinics of North America*, 19: 341–349

Bluebond-Langner, M. (1978) *The Private Worlds of Dying Children*, Princeton, NJ: Princeton University Press.

—— (Speaker) (1983) *The Secret Worlds of Dying Children* (Cassette Recording), Kings's College, London, Ontario.

Buckingham, R.W. (1989) *Care of the Dying Child*, New York: The Continuum Publishing Company.

Burnett, F.H. (1911) *The Secret Garden*, (Tasha Tudor, ill.), New York: J.B. Lippincott.

Cooper, J. (1978) *An Illustrated Encyclopedia of Traditional Symbols*, London: Thames and Hudson.

Di Leo, J.H. (1983) *Interpretation of Children's Drawings*, New York: Brunner/Mazel.

Furth, G. (1973) Impromptu paintings by terminally ill, hospitalized and healthy children: What can we learn from them? (Doctoral dissertation, Ohio State University, 1973). University Microfilms No. 73–3170.

—— (1981) 'The use of drawings made at significant times in one's life', in E. Kübler-Ross, *Living with Death and Dying* (pp. 63–94), New York: Macmillan.

—— (1988) *The Secret World of Drawings: Healing Through Art*, Boston, MA: Sigo Press.

Hammer, E. (1958) *The Clinical Application of Projective Drawings*, Springfield, IL: Charles C. Thomas.

—— (1985) 'Introduction and perspective', in A. Wohl & B. Kaufman, *Silent Screams and Hidden Cries: An Interpretation of Artwork by Children from Violent Homes* (pp. xiii–xvii), New York: Brunner/Mazel.

Herder Symbol Dictionary (1986) (B. Matthews, trans.), Wilmette, IL: Chiron Publications.

Jaffé, A. (ed.) (1979) *C.G. Jung Word and Image* (Bollingen Series XCVII), Princeton, NJ: Princeton University Press.

Jampolsky, G.G. & Taylor, P. (1978) *There is a Rainbow Behind Every Dark Cloud*, Tiburon, CA: Celestial Arts.

Jung, C.G. (1960) *The Structure and Dynamics of the Psyche*, (C.W. 8, 2nd edn) (R.F.C. Hull, trans.), Princeton, N.J.: Princeton University Press.

Kellog, R. (1969) *Analysing Children's Art*, Palo Alto, CA: Mayfield Publishing Company.

Keipenheuer, K. (1980) 'Spontaneous drawings of a leukemic child: An aid for a more comprehensive care of fatally ill children and their families', *Psychosomatische Medzin*, 9: 21–32.

Krementz, J. (1989) *How it Feels to Fight for Your Life*, Boston, MA: Little Brown and Company.

Krippner, S. (1989) 'Mythological aspects of death and dying', in A. Berger, P. Badham, A.H. Kutscher, J. Berger, M. Perry, & J. Beloff (eds), *Perspectives on Death and Dying: Cross Cultural and Multidisciplinary Views* (pp. 3–13), Philadelphia, PA: The Charles Press, Inc.

Kübler-Ross, E. (1969) *On Death and Dying*, New York: Macmillan.

—— (1979, May) A letter to a child – with cancer. (Available from Elisabeth Kübler-Ross Centre, S. Route 616, Head Waters, Virginia 24442).

—— (1981) *Living with Death and Dying*, New York: Macmillan.

—— (1982) *Remember the Secret*, Berkeley, CA: Celestial Arts.

—— (1983) *On Children and Death*, New York: Macmillan.

—— (Speaker) (1985) *Life, Death and the Dying Part 1*. Video Cassette #3A, Elisabeth Kübler-Ross Centre, Head Waters, Virginia.

Matter, D.E. & Matter, R.M. (1982) 'Developmental sequences in children's understanding of death with implications for counselors', *Elementary School Guidance and Counseling*, 17: 112–118.

Oaklander, V. (1978). *Windows to our Children*, Moab, UT: Real People Press.

O'Hanlon Nunn, R. (1987). *Tom's Remembrance* (R.T.Haynes, ill.), Loose Creek Missouri: The Westphalia Press.

Pert, C. with Dienstfrey, H. (1988) 'The Neuropeptide Network', In W. Pierpaoli and N.H. Spector (eds), *Neuroimmunomodulation: Interventions in Aging and Cancer*. First Stromboli Conference on Aging and Cancer, Annals of the New York Academy of Science, (521), 189–194.

Rando, T. (1984) *Grief, Dying and Death: Clinical Interventions for Caregivers*, Champaign, IL: Research Press.

Siegel, B. (1989) *Peace, Love and Healing*, New York: Harper & Row.

Stroebel, E., Stroebel, C.F., & Holland, M. (1980) *Kiddie QR – A Choice for Children©*, Hartford, CT: QR Institute.

Thompson, F. & Allan, J. (1987) 'Common symbols of children in art counselling', *Guidance and Counselling*, 2: 24–32.

Van Dongen-Melman, J. & Sanders-Woudstra, J. (1986) 'Psychosocial aspects of childhood cancer: A review of the literature', *Journal of Child Psychology and Psychiatry*, 27: 145–180.

Viorst, V. (1975) *Alexander and the Terrible, Horrible, No Good, Very Bad Day*, (Ray Cruz, ill.), New York: Atheneum.

von Franz, M. (1986) *On Dreams and Death*, (E. Kennedy & V. Brooks, trans.), Boston: Shambhala Publications, Inc. (original work published 1984).

White, E.B. (1952) *Charlotte's Web*, New York: Harper.

Wohl, A. & Kaufman, B. (1985) *Hidden Screams and Silent Cries*, New York: Brunner/Mazel.

Yin, R. (1989) *Case Study Research: Design and Methods* (Applied Social Research Methods Series Volume 5), Newbury Park, CA: Sage Publications.

Name index

Subject index

For Product Safety Concerns and Information please contact our EU representative GPSR@taylorandfrancis.com Taylor & Francis Verlag GmbH, Kaufingerstraße 24, 80331 München, Germany

Batch number: 10725971

Printed by Printforce, the Netherlands